Essent...

computer security

OTHER TITLES BY THE SAME AUTHOR

BP 418   Word 95 assistant

BP 421   Windows 95 assistant

BP 425   Microsoft Internet Explorer assistant

Essentials of computer security

by

Ian Sinclair

BERNARD BABANI (publishing) LTD
THE GRAMPIANS
SHEPHERDS BUSH ROAD
LONDON W6 7NF
ENGLAND

PLEASE NOTE

Although every care has been taken with the production of this book to ensure that any projects, designs, modifications and/or programs, etc., contained herewith, operate in a correct and safe manner and also that any components specified are normally available in Great Britain, the Publishers and Author(s) do not accept responsibility in any way for the failure (including fault in design) of any project, design, modification or program to work correctly or to cause damage to any equipment that it may be connected to or used in conjunction with, or in respect of any other damage or injury that may be so caused, nor do the Publishers accept responsibility in any way for the failure to obtain specified components.

Notice is also given that if equipment that is still under warranty is modified in any way or used or connected with home-built equipment then that warranty may be void.

© 1997 BERNARD BABANI (publishing) LTD

First Published – July 1997

British Library Cataloguing in Publication Data:

A catalogue record for this book is available from the British Library

ISBN 0 85934 422 3

Cover Design by Gregor Arthur
Cover Illustration by Adam Willis
Printed and Bound in Great Britain by Cox & Wyman Ltd.,
Reading

ABOUT THIS BOOK

Security of computers and their files in these days has become more and more of a problem, and not only for the large-scale commercial user of computers. Security embraces all the hazards that endanger your precious data, from power-supply failure through hard drive failure to theft of computers or files, and some users are more at risk than others from particular hazards.

This book deals with the problems of security for the small to medium size business or the home user of computers, and emphasises throughout that the main hazards are not the ones that provide newspaper headlines, but the often forgotten points such as limited life of a hard drive or the risks from fire or flood.

I hope that the advice contained here will ensure that many more computer users will never experience loss of data from any foreseeable cause. Though in the main, the user is assumed to be using Windows 95, descriptions of important methods applicable to Windows 3.1 are also included because of the large numbers of computer users who have not yet changed to the later version.

Ian Sinclair

Spring 1997

ABOUT THE AUTHOR

Ian Sinclair was born in 1932 in Tayport, Fife, and graduated from the University of St. Andrews in 1956. In that year, he joined the English Electric Valve Co. in Chelmsford, Essex, to work on the design of specialised cathode-ray tubes, and later on small transmitting valves and TV transmitting tubes.

In 1966, he became an assistant lecturer at Hornchurch Technical College, and in 1967 joined the staff of Braintree College of F.E. as a lecturer. His first book, "Understanding Electronic Components" was published in 1972, and he has been writing ever since, particularly for the novice in Electronics or Computing. The interest in computing arose after seeing a Tandy TRS80 in San Francisco in 1977, and of his 180 published books, about half have been on computing topics, starting with a guide to Microsoft Basic on the TRS80 in 1979.

He left teaching in 1984 to concentrate entirely on writing, and has also gained experience in computer typesetting, particularly for mathematical texts. He has recently visited Seattle to see Microsoft at work, and to remind them that he has been using Microsoft products longer than most Microsoft employees can remember.

ACKNOWLEDGEMENTS

I would like to thank the staff of Text 100 Ltd. for providing the Windows 3.1 and Windows 95 software on which this book has been based.

TRADEMARKS

Microsoft, MS-DOS, Windows, Windows 95 and NT are either registered trademarks or trademarks of Microsoft Corporation.

All other brand and product names used in this book are recognised as trademarks, or registered trademarks, of their respective companies.

CONTENTS

1. What does security mean? 1
   Total loss 2
   Losing files 3
   Maintenance 5
   Hacking 6
   Unauthorised copying 7

2. Physical security 8
   The computer site 8
   Theft 10
   Marking chips 12
   Disc maintenance 13
   File repairs 14
   Using SCANDISK with Windows 95 15
   Clearing out scrap 17

3. Floppy backup 20
   Backing up 20
   Simple backup 21
   Microsoft Backup 22
   Microsoft Backup on floppies 24
   Using a File Set 26
   Recovery 27
   Backup options 28
   Windows 3.1 backup 33
   Configuring MWBACKUP 34
   Making a Windows 3.1 backup 35
   Restoring files 37

4. Tape and other backups 40
   High-capacity floppies 40
   External hard drives 42
   QIC tape 43
   Other tape cartridges 47
   DAT and similar units 48
   Optical units 49
   Testing 52

5. Keeping backups safe 55
    Long-term storage 56
    Distributing copies 59
    Backup computers 59
    Erasure 60
    Windows 3.1 undelete 63

6. On-line security 66
    Common worries 66
    Using passwords 67
    How to be immune from hackers 68
    Internal security 70
    Using the Internet and Email 72
    Secure actions 73
    Email 74

7. Viruses 76
    Virus types 78
    Avoiding infection 80
    Windows 3.1 anti-virus 81
    Using Vsafe 84
    Viruses in documents 85

8. Power supply interruption 86
    Data at risk 86
    Frequent backups 87
    Uninterruptable power supplies (UPS) 88
    Types of UPS 88

Appendix A. Hard drive data recovery 91

Appendix B. Specialists 92

Appendix C. Anti-virus software for Windows 95 94

Index 95

1 What does security mean?

A dictionary definition of security as applied to computers is 'the safeguarding of computer systems against damage to hardware, program software or data software'.

The risks to the hardware are the usual hazards of fire, flood, theft and malicious damage. For large computers, an air-conditioning system must be present to ensure that temperature, humidity and dust are all controlled, and any failure of this system can eventually cause damage to the computer system The program and data software is also vulnerable to the same hazards as the hardware, and to several others in addition. Promises by the manufacturers that damaged software can be replaced in 24 hours should always be disregarded, and your security will be better if you work on the assumption that your software is irreplaceable.

Security, as applied to a computer, or a network of computers, has therefore a host of meanings that we do not use in connection with other valuable items. This is because the theft, or loss from fire, of the whole computer is only one aspect of the security problem, rather comparable to having your record player stolen but leaving your collection of discs.

Security of the hardware of the computer system is one obvious aspect, and the software is another. Less obvious is the risk that the software could be corrupted so that it did not run, making it impossible to gain access to your valuable data. Another risk is that the data is intentionally corrupted so that it contains items that you did not intend, such as payment of wages to an employee who does not exist. Your data might be sensitive, so that copying with a view to leaking information is another aspect of security that does not involve any change that you can detect.

Essentials of computer security

In addition, computer security is not simply an aspect of crime prevention. Your computer stores both programs and data on a hard drive, and any failure of that hard drive can mean the loss of all the programs and data that the drive contains. This calls for drive maintenance and for attention to backups, and, unlike theft, hard drive failure is, eventually, inevitable and difficult to insure against. In this book, we cover all these aspects of computer security in terms that will be familiar to any computer user or owner.

Total loss

Safeguards against the total loss of a computer are covered in detail in Chapter 2. Computer theft is mainly directed against offices where several computers are kept, and is, at least, a hazard that can be covered by insurance. That said, the conditions for insuring computers can be difficult to fulfil, and premiums can be high, particularly if the computers are visible through a window and located in a room with easy access. Schools are the easiest targets for computer theft, but computers located in offices are more likely to contain valuable chips (the main reason for theft) or equally valuable data.

Fire is another hazard which can also be covered to some extent by insurance, but insurance will not usually extend to the contents of a hard drive, which can be more valuable than the hardware itself. Fire prevention is a subject that could by itself fill a book much larger than this one, and the most obvious hints for reducing the risk are:

- Do not leave computers switched on when the office is unoccupied unless this is unavoidable (because the computers must be on-line).

- Do not keep paperwork around the computers

What does security mean?

- Do not place the computers in a room which has other heat-generating equipment (such as fax machines) running overnight.

Computers that are used at home can be difficult to insure. If you use such a machine for games only, it will often be covered by the normal house insurance policy, but if you use the computer for any form of business purpose many domestic insurers will refuse to cover it. If this might be a problem, sort it out now before you need to make a claim, because insurance policies do not always make it clear to what extent a computer might be covered. You may need to take much more insurance cover than you need because the policy that is used to cover a computer used at home is one aimed at office premises, and you might also be asked to make your home much more secure, with an approved burglar alarm.

Losing files

The loss of files is often more of a risk than the loss of a computer. You can go out and buy a computer or use mail-order to get one the following day, but your data may represent years of work which you cannot replace. Even your off-the-shelf programs can represent considerable effort, because modern programs allow you to modify their action (*customizing* them), and reinstalling a program will not replace the additions and amendments that you made unless you have a backup copy of the program as it existed on your hard drive. Consider, for example, how many changes you have made to your copy of Windows 95 since it was installed.

All of that brings us to the subject of backups. A dictionary defines a *backup* as a spare copy of a program or data, and this very important aspect of security is dealt with in Chapters 3 to 5. Backup is not done simply because of the

Essentials of computer security

possibility of theft of data or of the computer. The storage of data can **never** be totally trustworthy, whether it is on floppy discs or on a hard drive, and discs are particularly susceptible to damage from high temperatures and magnetic fields.

Obviously, magnetic discs should be kept in cool well-ventilated places, but the magnetic field hazard is not so obvious. Magnetic fields radiate from anything that contains magnets, so that discs should not be stored near powerful magnets, and that includes objects like loudspeakers. The most damaging type of magnetic fields, however, are fluctuating magnetic fields which you can get from electric motors, from monitors or TV receivers. The closer discs are kept to such devices, the greater the risk of corruption of the disc. Perhaps you might not notice any effect in a year, but at some stage, the magnetism might alter a vital portion of a disc, making the whole lot unusable.

- Any valuable program or data should therefore be backed up, and many commercial users maintain at least two backups, which are renewed at regular intervals. The time-honoured method that is used is called the grandfather, father, son principle.

This is most easily described by example. You save a valuable file, usually on a hard drive, and you make a backup, the father file. Next time the data is modified, you make another backup which becomes the father file, and the older backup becomes the grandfather file. The file you normally work on is the son file, usually held on the hard drive, and each time it is altered, a new backup is made and becomes the father, and the previous father version becomes the grandfather. This ensures that there are always backups of the most recent changes and one older version.

Software for small machines, particularly home computers, is generally off-the-shelf, and comparatively easy to replace, but

What does security mean?

it should nevertheless be backed up by copies unless it has been supplied on CD-ROM. If a program whose cost is a substantial fraction of the price of the hardware cannot be backed up (as a precaution against copying) or can be backed up only to a limited extent, it should not be used.

Corruption is another substantial worry, and unless you have experienced the sinking feeling that comes over you when you see a screen message to the effect that a file cannot be read, you may have given it little thought. A corrupted data file is not such a loss as a stolen or destroyed file but, unless you have advanced skills, it can be just as destructive.

A corrupted file can usually be extracted from a disc or hard drive and reinstated. Files of text are the easiest to recover, and there are several utility programs that will read whatever is on a corrupted disc and store it on anther disc to be sorted out. When the lost file was a text file, it is easy then to read or print the recovered version and check for alteration.

This type of recovery action is not nearly so simple when the file was not a simple text file. In other words, if your corrupted file was from a word-processor, you can probably recover the text, but if it came from a spreadsheet, a database, an accounts program — virtually anything other than a word-processor — you might not be able to read the recovered file. This makes backup doubly important for such files.

Maintenance

The failure of a hard drive is inevitable, as inevitable as a breakdown of your car. It may not happen for years, and the rapid changes in computers over the last twenty years have ensured that it is not a problem that many have encountered, because the hard drive is usually replaced along with the computer before they have attained a ripe old age.

Essentials of computer security

Hard drives are now very reliable, and you should certainly get 3 or more years of use without problems, but that's an average, like the average lifespan of a person. You will normally safeguard against total loss of a hard drive by making backups, but you should also practice maintenance of the hard drive, using utility programs at intervals to check that the disk is working correctly. This aspect of security is dealt with in Chapter 2, and should not be neglected. Very often, a hard drive does not fail suddenly and catastrophically, but starts to lost data in a small way at first, becoming more serious as it ages. This type of slow failure can be detected by using disc utility programs, and the reports from these programs can be a useful guide to the need to replace a hard drive and copy all the data from the old drive on to the new one.

Hacking

The word 'hacking' has been used extensively in connection with theft or corruption of data and programs, and, like many other crimes, is not quite so common as you might think. Hacking means unauthorised access to your computer by remote control, and is possible only if your computer:

- is connected to others through telephone or other accessible lines, and
- is running a program that allows controlling signals to be sent to it through these lines, and
- is left unattended.

If you have no modem to connect to telephone lines, you are at no risk of hacking. Similarly, even if you have a modem, the risk of hacking exists only if you keep the modem switched on along with the computer and run them both unattended with software that permits access.

What does security mean?

The risk is highest for computers that must be kept on-line to other machines, exchanging confidential data such as bank statements, medical records, etc. This considerably narrows the risk, and in general there are safeguards available to users of such high-risk machines. The user of a stand-alone computer is not at such risk.

Unauthorised copying

Unauthorised copying is a much greater hazard than hacking, and is often mistaken for hacking. If your computer is on a network, or stands in an unoccupied office, it is simple for anyone who knows the machine to make a copy of any file on your hard drive. When the machine is in a network, the files on your hard drive may be shared on the network and can be copied from any other machine on the network. Unlike a hacker who is to some extent working blind, the unauthorised copier knows what to look for and where to find it.

Even if your machine is not networked (and nowadays this is quite rare in offices), an open office makes it easy to copy files on a floppy. Many offices are very vulnerable to this type of action, and investigators of software theft usually assume that any such copying is an inside job, because insiders are most likely to know what files might be worth copying. It is also easy for an insider to leave a message of the 'Kilroy was here' variety to make it seem as if a hacker had been at work.

2 Physical security

The computer site

The security of a computer with regard to theft, fire or flooding is very much affected by where the computer is kept. Other things being equal, a computer in a basement is more likely to be affected by flooding, and one on a top floor is more likely to be affected by fire. A computer room that is visible from outside the building is more at risk from theft because the value of its contents can be assessed easily.

You do not necessarily have many options on the siting of your computer(s), and you may have to make the best of whatever is available. If the computer room is in a basement, the risk of fire can be minimised by making sure that fire is unlikely to start in the computer room or elsewhere in the basement. The risk of theft is usually lower in a basement situation because it should be easier to ensure that the computers are not visible from outside, and it should also be easier to ensure that unauthorised entry is difficult. This leaves only the threat of flooding, and though nothing can protect from a really catastrophic flood such as can occur when a river bursts its banks, it should be possible to guard against flooding from burst water pipes or from water entry after a storm.

If the site is an old one, enquire if flooding has happened before, and, if so, what pattern it took. It may be possible to guard against similar flooding, though some advice from local authorities or consulting civil engineers may be needed. Water authorities may be able to help in preventing damage caused by water leakage or bursts from supply pipes. The main point is that flooding is a common hazard and there are well-known methods of minimising damage.

Physical security

One important safeguard is to fit flood alarms which will sound when the floor becomes more moist than normal. These alarms can be set to alert a member of staff (remotely, if necessary), or simply to sound a siren or flash lights. For home computers, small versions of flood alarms (intended for use under washing machines) are obtainable.

Fire is another hazard whose danger can often be greatly reduced by planning. The Fire Brigade will be pleased to inspect your computer room and warn of fire hazards, and the use of smoke and fire alarms is a second line of defence. One point to watch is that the use of automatic sprinklers might be as damaging as the effects of a fire, and this is a point on which Fire Brigade advice should be sought — you should certainly not disable sprinklers in a computer room without notifying all concerned, including local authorities and insurance company.

The risk of fire originating in a computer room should be tackled first. As noted in Chapter 1, try to avoid any build-up of paper. Despite hopeful prophesies of a 'paperless office', paper seems to build up in computer rooms, and tidy working should be established. Sources of flame should be banned, so that the normal no-smoking rule should be accompanied by warnings about flammable items.

The list of items that are not allowed into a computer room should be almost identical to the list used for aircraft security, and all products that are used for such purposes as monitor screen cleaning should be stored elsewhere and used only when the computers are not switched on. Monitors contain points at high voltage, and there is always a risk that sparking in a monitor could ignite flammable vapour. The same hazard, incidentally, exists in the home, and the combination of hair-sprays and other flammable sprays with large colour TV receivers is a form of accident just waiting to happen.

Essentials of computer security

The fire risk is greatly increased when equipment is allowed to run unattended overnight. If a night-watchman is employed, the risk is reduced, but it is better if nothing runs unattended if at all possible. Some fax machines seem to run hot, and since they are normally left working all night and at weekends they should be kept in a place that is separated from the main computer room, preferably a well-ventilated fireproof cupboard.

Theft

Theft is now the most common hazard for computers in offices. At one time, it was a considerable safeguard to ensure that the computers were out of sight of any casual visitor to the office, but nowadays any thief knows that virtually all offices use computers, and that some offices, such as newspaper premises, are likely to have a large number of well-equipped machines.

It is still useful if the computer room is not easily visible, but security against theft needs rather more to be done, and security is almost impossible if theft is committed with the aid of an insider who knows the most valuable items, where everything is, and how to disable alarms.

Many computer thefts at the time of writing are committed with the aim of stripping processor and memory chips from the machines. These components are difficult to trace and easy to sell (any small advertisement in the computer journals), and of high value. Computers are now of such standardised design that it is easy for a thief to locate these chips. Further advice on chip theft follows later in this chapter.

The first line of defence against theft of, or from, computers lies in making the computer room secure. Obviously it should be capable of locking, but since most internal office doors are

Physical security

flimsy, locking is only a defence against opportunist theft. Once again, you should be prepared to take advice from experts, and if the risk is high in your area, you may need to fit more substantial doors with good locks, and have windows wired and reinforced. Such precautions are not really applicable to machines used at home, but a stout front door is desirable in any home.

The second line of defence is alarms, and alarm systems should be of the type that will alert the Police rather than just a staff member. Since nothing warm should be moving around in the locked computer room, infra-red (IR) motion detectors are a useful form of alarm. More than one IR detector is needed to avoid blind spots. If the building is old, remember that the more sensitive forms of IR detectors can be triggered by mice.

Bolting down computer frames to their tables is another line of defence which is often used in schools and colleges. This is seldom useful for offices because it is the chips rather than the whole machines that are the main target of office theft. Bolting down is also a relatively cheap and useful form of defence for home computers, but only if you can install it yourself.

The last line of defence is to install alarms within the computer casings. These will operate if the machine is moved or opened, and they can be disabled if such movement or opening is needed by authorised staff. Such alarms are very much a last-ditch effort, but they can be enough to deter theft when time is short, and certainly should deter the opportunist thief. Appendix B lists addresses for firms that specialise in alarms for PCs.

Do not allow yourself to be persuaded into any form of disabling system that is claimed to prevent a stolen computer from being used by anyone else. These do not deter chip theft,

Essentials of computer security

and it is foolish to assume that professional computer thieves will be unable to deal with such systems.

All of these defences are totally useless if you cannot trust your staff. A few words of inside information from a staff member allows any form of security to be breached, and if keys, codes and other unlocking devices can be stolen or copied, theft is almost impossible to prevent. Consider having more than one layer of trust, so that only one or two people have complete knowledge of the alarm system and other precautions.

Marking chips

Until chip manufacturers agree on a way of coding valuable chips so that they can be identified, theft of processor and memory chips will be the most common form of hardware security problem. Until that day, you can assist by marking all the main chips yourself, using any of the ultra-violet visible pens that are available.

This means that you have to be able to identify these chips for yourself, but the manual for the computer should assist by illustrating locations. You need only put a post-code or other identifier on each chip (or SIMM chip board for memory), and in a few places around the inside of the computer. Prices of hard drives are so low that these are seldom stolen, but they are worth marking just in case they are stolen for the data files that they contain. Marking needs to be done in an inconspicuous position because it can be seen in daylight or under fluorescent lights. Do not, however, attempt to open sealed units such as hard drives.

The rapidly-decreasing cost of memory at the time of writing has reduced the amount of thefts aimed at memory boards, but processors in the Pentium 160 class are still (literally) worth their weight in gold. They should always be marked,

Physical security

because if they are stolen they have to be sold on quickly (as their value drops immediately a new version is announced). The down side of this is that, though marking allows you to identify your chips, it may still be impossible to find them.

Chip thieves are professionals — they know what is valuable and where to find it, and in many cases their remarkable speed of working suggests internal help. A combination of vigilance and good physical security is the only safeguard.

Disk maintenance

Apart from inner-town areas, a hazard that is far more of a menace than all computer crime is loss of data because of faults in a hard drive. Backing up is essential, but unless files can be recovered quickly, the time spent on recovery may be enough to cripple your activities for too long. The remainder of this chapter is therefore devoted to the problem of keeping a hard drive in good condition and of checking for faults. This advice will be found in any good text on hard drive use, but its security aspect is often forgotten.

The most common problem that can arise during use is 'lost clusters'. These arise from a file that has become fragmented, meaning that it has portions stored in different places on the drive. A cluster is a group of data bytes and clusters are lost when the information that leads from one portion to another becomes erased. Such fragmented files are often unwanted, and have been deleted from the directory, but because they do not appear on any directory display you cannot remove them from the drive or do anything with them.

These lost clusters often occur after you have had an extensive session of deleting old files. They can be a nuisance in two ways. One is that they take up disk space, the other is that they can become cross-linked with other files, causing corruption.

Essentials of computer security

The main diagnostic and repair utilities for lost clusters are CHKDSK and SCANDISK. CHKDSK is the older utility of Windows 3.1, and if you are using Windows 95 you will have the later SCANDISK version which you should use in preference.

Looking first at CHKDSK, you can use this purely as a diagnostic either from DOS or from Windows. Switching to DOS and using CHKDSK alone will search the hard drive, or whatever disk is currently being used, for faults, and report on bad portions or lost pieces of files.

After CHKDSK has run you will see a report on lost bits of files, referred to as *allocation units*. If lost allocation units are reported, you can opt either to convert them to files that can be read (if they contain text), or to remove them altogether. These lost units are usually from deleted files, and can be removed. Any report on bad portions of a hard drive should be taken as a warning that the drive may be on its way out, because when bad portions are detected they are locked out of use by CHKDSK. This ensures that such portions are not used and not checked again, so that later bad-portion notices indicate drive deterioration.

File repairs

The version of the CHKDSK command that will fix faults as well as diagnosing them is CHKDSK /F. You must **never** use this form from Windows, only from DOS. If you use CHKDSK on a modern DOS you will be reminded that SCANDISK is much more comprehensive and useful, and can be used from Windows 95.

To use CHKDSK from DOS you must first shut down Windows. This assumes that you are using Windows 3.1 or 3.11, because if you are using Windows 95 you will have SCANDISK available and should use it.

Physical security

Use the DOS command CD \DOS (or CD \MSDOS if this is the name of your DOS directory) Type the command CHKDSK /F and press the ENTER key.

Wait until the message appears about any lost portions of files. You may be asked if you want to save these bits in a new file. This is useful only if the bits are of text files and if you need them. If you do not opt to save the pieces in a file they will be deleted.

Using SCANDISK with Windows 95

If you are using Windows 95, you can check the state of your hard drive by using the more advanced utility SCANDISK.

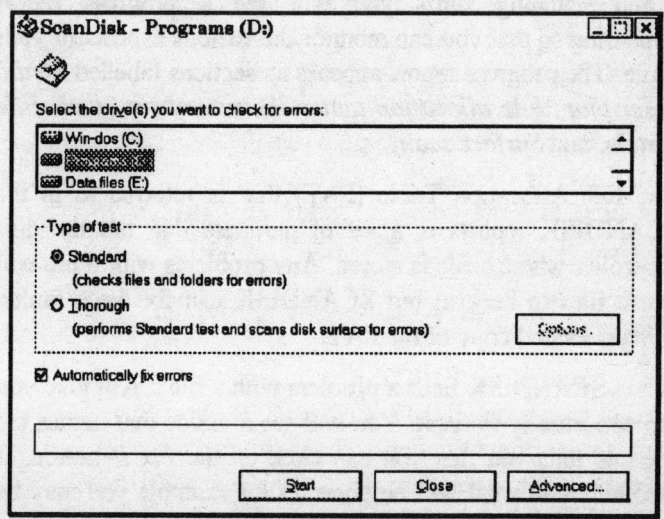

Click on the Start button, and move the pointer successively to Programs, Accessories, and System Tools. Click on the ScanDisk item. You can then select the drive — the (main) hard drive will be selected as a default.

Essentials of computer security

Choose the type of scan that is needed from the options of *Standard* or *Thorough*. The *Thorough* test can take a considerable time. Make sure that there is a tick against the box labelled *Automatically Fix Errors*. Click on the *Start* button of the SCANDISK panel to carry out the scan.

A thorough scan is a lengthy business. Fortunately, you do not need to use SCANDISK very often, usually after you have been deleting a large number of files. The longest wait is for a surface scan. You should carry out a surface scan only at intervals, perhaps twice a year. A hard drive will usually start to suffer from surface defects only after a considerable running time, and reports on surface faults are a good indication that the hard drive should be replaced.

When scanning starts you will see a progress report appearing so that you can monitor the various aspects of your drive .The progress report appears as sections labelled *Media descriptor, File allocation tables, Directory structure, File system,* and *Surface scan*.

The File Allocation Table (FAT) that is referred to in the SCANDISK reports is a set of numbers that tell the disc controller where a file is stored. Any problems with these will cause files to be lost, but SCANDISK can fix these faults, using a second copy of the FAT.

When SCANDISK finds a problem with a file it will give you the opportunity to fix it. You will see a notice that names the file and tells you that you can click on the *Fix It* button. It also tells you what will be done — for example you may be told that the damaged part of the file will be removed and the file altered so that it can be used. Simply removing damage will not, except for a text file, result in a file that is useable.

Usually when SCANDISK finds a damaged file, it's a file that you had deleted, and you don't need to recover it. You may get reports of cross-linked files that involve files that you

Physical security

do want to keep, but remember that repaired files are not always useful — it all depends on the type of files. You can look at the filename to determine what type of file is being reported.

If the file is one that is of text, removing damage and patching up the file will result in something that you can read and use. If the file is a program file of the COM or EXE variety you cannot recover it in this way. Never attempt to run a program file that has been damaged. If there are any faults, they are usually in the File Allocation Tables (FAT), directory structure, or File system of the disc. The illustration here shows a final report that proves that the drive is in perfect order — and this is what you can expect on a drive in good condition.

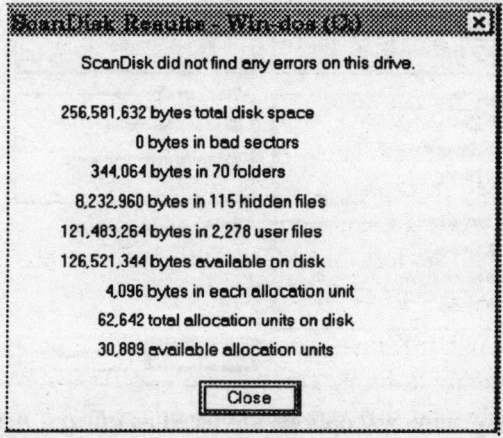

Clearing out scrap

Often the use of SCANDISK will find fragments of files that cannot be identified. These usually result from some deletion actions in the past, and because they take up disc space you would prefer them to be removed.

Essentials of computer security

There is a faint possibility, however, that this was something you did not mean to delete, and so SCANDISK gives you the chance to gather all the bits up into a file, give it a name, and make it accessible. This is useful only when the bits are mainly of text, because you can edit a text file. Other file types are not usually useful, because they will not usually be recognised by the program (such as a spreadsheet) that uses the files.

The main panel of SCANDISK contains a button labelled Advanced. This provides a new panel with some useful options.

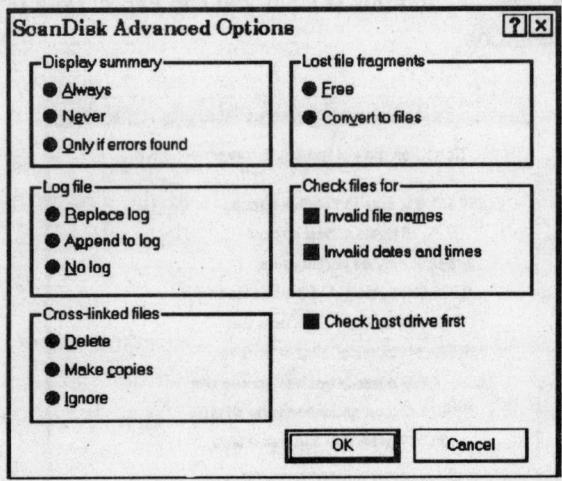

The display summary options are listed as *always*, *never* and *if errors found*. The default of *always* ensures that you get news, whether good or bad. Another default is to convert lost file fragments into files so that you can see if they contain anything useful.

The log file (which is a text file that contains a note of the result) can be replaced each time unless you suspect that the

Physical security

disk is deteriorating and want to compare successive files. The *Check files for* section uses the default of *invalid file names*, and this is all you normally need.

The option for making copies of cross-linked files is useful. These are files that have become connected, and this option offers some chance of recovering information.

The other aspect of hard drive maintenance is defragmentation, but this does not have any security implications, and you can find details of the action in any good book on Windows 95. Briefly, fragmentation means that a file is stored in fragments that are scattered around the hard drive. This fragmentation arises because when a new file is saved, it will be placed into any portions of the hard drive that have become available because of older files being deleted. A new large file will therefore take portions of the hard drive that previously were used by several small files, making this file fragmented.

Fragmentation has two effects. One is that the system takes longer to save and load the file, because it has to be pieced together from several different locations. The other is that there is always a risk that the codes which guide the computer to the locations will become corrupted. Defragmentation will read and re-save files, one by one, ensuring that each file is one continuous entity (a *contiguous* file). You should carry out defragmentation at the same time as you use SCANDISK.

3 Floppy backup

Backing up

A backup copy is one that you hope will be like an insurance policy, something that you will not need to call upon but which you will be very grateful for **when** (not if) the time comes. You should keep backup copies of all files other than temporary files, and if your computing is part of your business you should keep a strict grandfather – father – son system going, as explained in Chapter 1.

If your computing and backup requirements are more modest, so that backing up on floppies is adequate for your needs, you will have to think carefully about **what** material you back up. Programs that have been installed from CD-ROM need not be backed up, because the CD-ROM format is itself much more secure than the conventional magnetic disc. You might also feel that programs that have been supplied on floppies and installed on the hard drive need no further backup.

The most important backups, then, are the data files, such as are generated by your accounts program, spreadsheet, database, word-processor and others, all of which you generate for yourself and which cannot be replaced if they are wiped, either from carelessness or by hard drive failure. If this data can be backed up on to a reasonable number of floppies then there is no need to go for more elaborate and costly backup systems as detailed in the following chapters. What constitutes a reasonable number of floppies very much depends on how much time you can devote to making the backups and how often you create them. It depends also on how you intend to store these backups, and that's something we shall return to in Chapter 5.

Floppy backup

Simple backup

The most straightforward type of backup is simply to copy data files from the hard drive to a floppy. Some programs assist in this action by providing suitable routines. For example, Word for Windows 7 contains a macro called *Auto Backup* which will create a floppy copy of a document each time a save action is used — you will get a warning message if there is no floppy in the drive at the time. If you are skilled in writing macros you can write such routines for other programs that have a macro facility, or you can copy macro routines that you see published in magazines such as PC Plus.

If your programs do not contain any provision for macros, you will need to use the conventional methods of Windows. Using Windows 95 you can select the files and drag them to the floppy drive icon (assuming that a floppy disc has been placed in the drive). A variation on this is to place the floppy icon into the *Send To* folder. You can then select files, click on File — Send To, and then on the floppy drive icon. Using Windows 3.1 you can perform the copying action using File Manager. If the number of files requires more than one floppy you will be advised when to change discs.

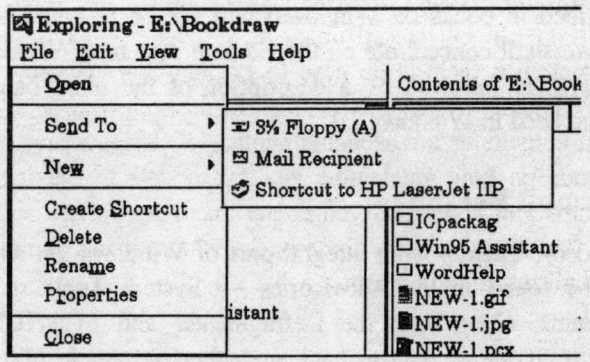

Essentials of computer security

Windows 3.1 also contained a macro system called Recorder which, though not entirely straightforward to set up, allowed actions such as saving selected files to the floppy drive to be automated so that you could mark the files and press a key or key combination to carry out the backup action. If you now use Windows 95 but previously used Windows 3.1, the Recorder program may still be on your hard drive. If your computer came equipped with Windows 95 the Recorder program will not be included. If you use Windows 3.1 and want to experiment with Recorder, see any good book on Windows 3.1. A macro system called *Flute* is available for Windows 95 but is not built into Windows 95. The use of macros requires some knowledge and understanding of the system, and it is difficult to find any texts on macro use.

The advantage of simple backup systems is that the files can be read by other users and are immediately available to you because they are in the normal format. This, however, imposes the usual limits of 1.4 Mbyte per floppy. You can save space by using the DriveSpace action on the floppies, but since this makes a floppy that cannot be read by other users unless they also have the DriveSpace facility, you might as well use the Microsoft Backup program to get the equivalent of about 4 Mbyte on each floppy. For these reasons, the use of DriveSpace on floppies (which is described in books on Windows) will not be repeated here, and we shall concentrate on the Backup system of Windows 95. This is followed by a description of the older backup system used in Windows 3.1.

Microsoft Backup

Microsoft Backup is an integral part of Windows 95, and it can be found in the Accessories — System Tools set of programs, along with the Defragmenter and SCANDISK utilities. It allows you to back up either the whole of your

Floppy backup

software or your selected data in compressed form on floppies, tapes, other computers on a network, or removable hard drives. You can also use it to compare a backup file with the original, and to retrieve files from backed-up form.

The process is automatic once it has been started, though if you use floppies you will need to change discs at intervals – about 4 Mbyte can be saved on each floppy. Only a few types of tape drive (such as the Colorado Jumbo) are recognised by *Backup*, and if you use other types you will need to use the software that comes with the backup system.

Backups that are made using this system are very tightly compressed, so that if you back up to floppies, these floppies cannot be read except by using the *Restore* action of Backup. Since Backup is part of Windows 95, however, it allows you to read your data even if the computer has been stolen and you need to use another machine. Provided that the replacement machine runs Windows 95, you can recover your data and use it. There is no guarantee that data recorded by using Backup of Windows 95 will be readable using later versions of Windows (or by Windows NT), but it is highly likely that compatibility would be preserved and in any case, you could recover your files before changing to the later version of Windows and then back them up again after making the change. You would, in any case, back up all files before changing your operating system.

Compared to the earlier backup systems used on Windows 3.0 and 3.1, the later system is much easier to use and is very much more reliable. This latter point is particularly important, because if it is difficult to recover data from a backup, the backup is not particularly useful. Any backup system should be tested — you should not wait for a catastrophe to find out how to recover data.

Essentials of computer security

Microsoft Backup on floppies

You do not need to select files in advance. Click the *Start* button of Windows 95, followed by *Programs*, *Accessories* and *System Tools*. From the *System Tools* set, click *Backup*. The main *Microsoft Backup* panel will appear, as illustrated here. The Backup panel is selected by default, and the other two tabs are labelled as *Restore* and *Compare*.

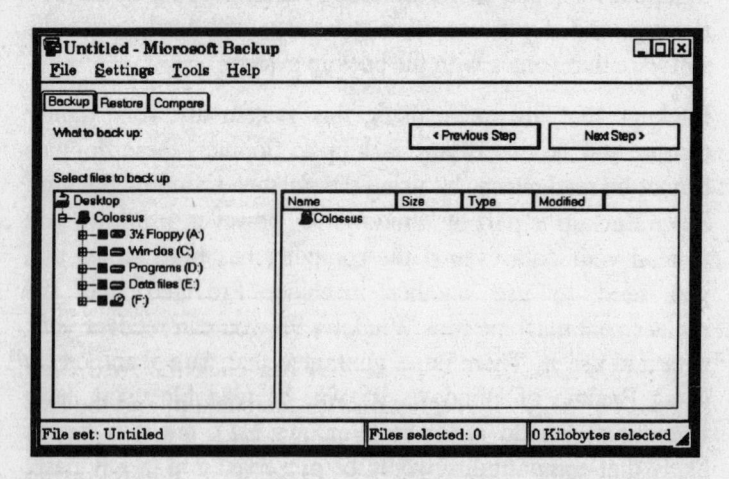

```
Untitled - Microsoft Backup                        _ □ ×
File  Settings  Tools  Help
[Backup] Restore  Compare
What to back up:              < Previous Step    Next Step >

Select files to back up
  Desktop                 Name      Size   Type   Modified
  ⊟─ Colossus              Colossus
     ⊞─■  3½ Floppy (A:)
     ⊞─■  Win-dos (C:)
     ⊞─■  Programs (D:)
     ⊞─■  Data files (E:)
     ⊞─■  (F:)

File set: Untitled           Files selected: 0   0 Kilobytes selected
```

We shall look later at the options that can be used for backup, recovery and comparison, and concentrate for the moment on the backing up action alone.

Backup, as illustrated here, initially shows a list of folders and files in Explorer format, with a small box next to each name. You can click this box to place a tick into it and so select it.

Selecting a box for a drive will automatically select all of the folders and files on that drive. Selecting a box for a folder name will select for backup all the files in that folder. You can also click the normal Explorer-type box with its [+] sign to see a list of files and sub-folders and so select file names

Floppy backup

individually, as illustrated earlier. If a large number of files is selected the process can take several minutes.

You can also name and save a selection so that it can be repeated later without the need to select individual items. Note that selecting a folder will allow for files in that folder to change, so that if you have a folder named, for example, *archive*, you can select that folder to back up any files that have been placed there.

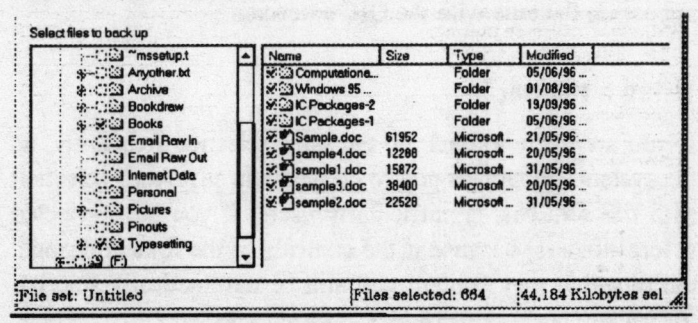

Select files to back up				
~mssetup.t	Name	Size	Type	Modified
Anyother.txt	Computationa...		Folder	05/06/96 ...
Archive	Windows 95 ...		Folder	01/08/96 ...
Bookdraw	IC Packages-2		Folder	19/09/96 ...
Books	IC Packages-1		Folder	05/06/96 ...
Email Raw In	Sample.doc	61952	Microsoft...	21/05/96 ...
Email Raw Out	sample4.doc	12286	Microsoft...	20/05/96 ...
Internet Data	sample1.doc	15872	Microsoft...	31/05/96 ...
Personal	sample3.doc	38400	Microsoft...	20/05/96 ...
Pictures	sample2.doc	22528	Microsoft...	31/05/96 ...
Pinouts				
Typesetting				
(F:)				
File set: Untitled		Files selected: 664		44,184 Kilobytes sel

When files have been selected, you can click the *Next Step* button. This selects a destination for the backup, and the two most likely are **floppy drive** or (if you have a tape backup) **tape**. We shall deal with tape backups in the following chapter. If you are using floppies, make sure that a formatted blank (or spare) floppy is inserted into the drive, and then click the *Start Backup* button. If the floppy contains files you will be reminded that the backup action will wipe out these files.

You will be asked to type a filename for your backup, and a useful type of filename is the date (such as 8JUN96) along with an indication of the contents (DATA, SYSTEM, PROGS, etc.). When you have done this and clicked the backup will start. If you are using floppies you will be prompted to change discs at intervals. You should label these floppies in sequence, as they will need to be inserted in the

Essentials of computer security

same order when you restore the contents — you will also need to insert the last floppy when you backup so that the list of files can be read from it.

Backup will indicate its progress by showing what percentage of the data has been backed up, both in terms of files numbers and in terms of size. The filename that appears on the floppies will use the QIC extension, so that if you provided a filename of 12NOV96WordFiles this name will appear on the tape with the QIC extension.

Using a File set

If you are likely to back up the same selection frequently, as the system encourages you to do, you can save your selection as a *file set*. This is particularly useful if you have selected several folders, because if the contents of the folders change, the files that they contain will still be automatically selected for backup because the folder has been selected.

The file set can be saved **after** you have selected a destination for the backup by clicking File — Save As in the menu, and providing a filename for the selection. This is saved as a file of type SET and it can be obtained subsequently by using File — Open File Set the next time you make a backup. Make sure that the name you use for the file set is one that reminds you of the contents — you will see the contents appearing as a selection when you make another backup using the same file set.

A file set for *Full System Backup* (FSB) is provided along with Backup, and it can be loaded in when you are asked to select files. An FSB will backup all of the files on the hard drive, including the important Windows registry files, so that you should make at least one backup of this type if you have a tape drive or a removable hard drive.

Floppy backup

The size of the FSB, normally 250 Mbyte or more, makes it unlikely that you will want to use floppies for this purpose. You can decrease the size of the FSB set by removing all data files and, if necessary, all program files other than the Windows set from the set. You will be asked to confirm any change to the FSB set.

Once you have selected files or used a file set, and specified the destination for backup (floppy or tape) you are ready to make the backup as described earlier, providing a filename for the backup disc files.

Recovery

Data recovery is the other main part of the Microsoft Backup program. When you click on the Restore tab of the Backup panel you will be asked to click on the source of the backed up files, and you can select the A: drive if you are using floppies — the usual alternative will be Tape, but only if you have a tape unit fitted.

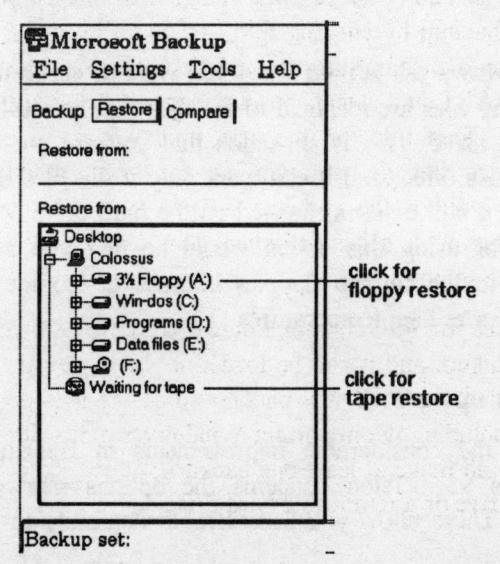

27

Essentials of computer security

When you indicate that you want to restore from a floppy, the **last** floppy in the backup set should be in the drive — if you have used any other floppy you will be prompted to insert the last of the set. The filename and contents list will be read from this, so that when you click the *Restore Now* button you will see the contents of the backup discs appear. The default system is to restore these to the folders from which they were backed up, and this will then be done — you can specify to restore just one file, or a selection of files or folders, as you please. See the following section on *Options* if you want to restore backed up data to other folders or drives.

Note that if you have **not** placed the last floppy of the set into the drive, the filename will be read, but not the full contents of the set. You will be asked to place the last disc of a backup set into the A: drive before Backup can display the full contents. Once the files are displayed, you can select the ones you want to restore, and you will then be asked to insert the discs in order — you cannot start halfway through a set even if you know that the files which you want are in the last few discs.

The *Compare* tab is used when you want to check that your backed up files are identical to the files that are still held on the hard drive. This is an action that you are not likely to need to use often, and it can work only if the files that were backed up still exist unchanged on the hard drive. A typical reason for using this action would be that you suspected damage to the backup floppies because of storage near to magnets or at high temperatures.

Backup options

One of the considerable improvements in Backup in its Windows 95 version concerns the options that you can specify. These allow you considerable flexibility in the way

Floppy backup

that you use backup, and also, because the options can be set before creating a file set, you can ensure that the conditions for backup or restore using a file set are always as you want them. One point to watch is that when you alter options, these alterations will remain in force until you change them again. If options are saved as part of a file set, these will over-rule any options that you are using for backing up without a file set. For example, you might make backups of files to be archived, and specify that a backup does not erase previously saved files. For routine backups, such as the FSB, you would normally want each backup to replace the earlier one.

The Settings — Options menu allows you to specify the options for general use and for the three main actions of *Backup*, *Restore* and *Compare*. These are detailed below.

The *General* options boxes provide for turning on audible prompts and for overwriting old status log files. Both of these can normally be ticked, unless there is some particular reason for retaining old log files. The status log files keep a note of each backup type of action that is carried out, and you would normally want to retain only the most recent file.

The *Backup* option panel contains a box which is labelled *Quit Backup after operation is finished*, and this can be ticked if you want to resume normal working as soon as possible after making a backup. If you are likely to use several backup actions in sequence, leave this box unticked, as the illustration (overleaf) shows.

Note, however, that some actions (such as automatically backing up Word files, or the use of Windows Explorer on the A: drive, will not be possible while Backup is active with the A: drive selected. If you see messages to the effect that the A: drive does not exist or is unavailable, this is because the floppy drive is tied up to Backup and is not available for other uses.

Essentials of computer security

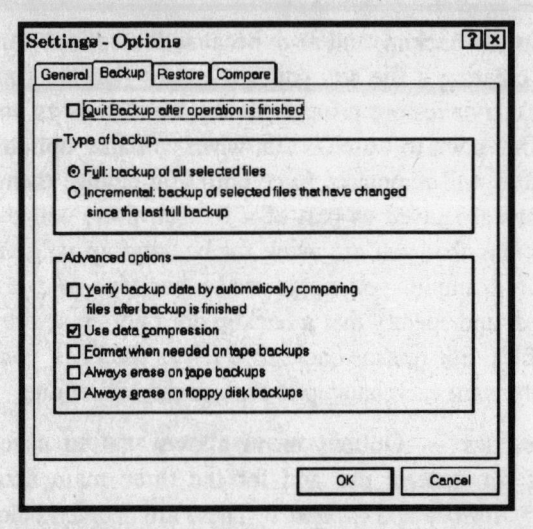

The *Type of Backup* options allow you to choose between making a full backup on all selected files and making an incremental backup only of files that have changed since the last full backup.

A *Full backup*, as the name suggests, backs up the files completely, so that they can be restored to the state they were in at the time of the backup. An *Incremental backup* backups only the changes in files and it can be made only after you have, at some stage, made a full backup of the same. This action should be reserved for specialised purposes, because it does **not** back up new files that have been added to folders, only changes in files that were previously backed up.

You must clear the *Always Erase on Tape Backup* option box (see later) before you add an incremental backup to a tape that contains an existing full backup. When you recover files, both the full backup *and* the incremental backup must be present. This makes incremental backup a choice that few users are likely to make.

Floppy backup

The *Advanced* section of the backup options has four option boxes. The *Verify backup* data box will automatically carry out a file comparison between the backup copy and the original and report on any differences. This is comforting if you are trying out Backup for the first time, but it can be too time-consuming for everyday use.

The box labelled *Use Data Compression* should be ticked, particularly if you are backing up to floppies, because it allows Backup to make full use of the available storage space. The option to *Format if necessary on tape backup* provides for using unformatted discs (or tape), and can save some time that would otherwise be spent in formatting a set of floppies.

The option of *Always erase on tape backup* allows the same tape to be used over and over again for a full backup, and must not be used if you want to make incremental backups on the same tape. The last option is *Always erase on floppy disk backup*, and this also is usually desirable unless you want to avoid the possibility of wiping a disc by mistake. If you want to add new backup selections to existing discs, you must not tick this last option.

The *Restore* options follow a similar pattern. The main option is *Quit Restore after operation is finished*, and you will probably want to tick this option because it is unlikely that you will want to carry out one restore action immediately following another.

You can also choose whether to restore backup files to the *Original location* (the default), to an *alternative location*, or to an *alternative location, into a single folder (directory)*. The use of an alternative location allows you, for example, to place all of your files on a new hard drive (added in parallel with the original), and the use of a single folder allows a set

Essentials of computer security

of files to be restored from a backup so that you can find them all without having to search through a set of folders.

The options to restore to new locations also avoids some problems, notably when you suspect that the hard drive is failing and that the files may not copy correctly to the hard drive. Restoring does not, of course, wipe the backup files from the floppies or tape, so that there is no risk of losing files if they are restored to an unreliable hard drive, but there is a risk that you might suspect the quality of the backups rather than that of the drive you restored them to.

The *Advanced* section of the Restore options provides first for verifying restored data against the backup copy, so checking that the hard drive now contains files that are identical to those held on the backup. The other options concern what happens when files are restored to folders that already contain the original files. These options are *Never overwrite files*, *Overwrite older files only*, or *Overwrite files*.

The first of these options is the safest, ensuring that if your hard drive contains a more up-to-date version of a file it will not be replaced by the older version that was backed up. The second option allows file dates to be compared, and will use the backup files only if they are more recent than the files on the hard drive. This would be unusual. The last option will replace existing files of the same name on the hard drive by the files on the backup discs, but you can opt for a prompt message to appear (with details of file name and date) each time a file is to be overwritten.

The *Compare* options start with the usual *Quit after operation is finished*. The other file comparison options follow the same pattern as the Restore options, using *Original location*, *Alternate location*, and *Alternate location, single folder (directory)*.

Floppy backup

The Settings menu of Backup also provides *for Drag and Drop* and for *File Filtering*. The *Drag and Drop* options allow you to specify how you want Backup to proceed when you have the Backup program displayed as an icon and you have selected files and dragged them to the Backup icon.

These options are to *Run Backup Minimized*, to *Confirm Operation before Beginning*, and to *Quit after Backup is Completed*.

File filtering allows you to specify file types (in the form of extension letters) that you want to exclude from a backup, or to exclude files on the basis of date. This is seldom needed if you use the more flexible system of file sets as described earlier.

Windows 3.1 backups

Though at the time of writing Windows 95 is well-established, a large number of computer users are still working with Windows 3.1 or 3.11, possibly from choice, but more often because of the use of older computers which are not fast enough or contain insufficient memory for Windows 95 use. The following section is a brief description of the older form of backup system (as distinct from simple copying actions) used in Windows 3.1. This is not as well-developed as the system used in Windows 95.

The main backup program for files running under Windows 3.1 is MWBACKUP. If you cannot find any trace of this file on your system you will have to install it. The files for MWBACKUP are **not** included with the Windows 3.1 distribution floppies, but with MS-DOS 6.22, and they should have been installed from the MS-DOS distribution disks. Consult any good text on MS-DOS to find how to locate and install these files.

Essentials of computer security

Do **not** try to use backup programs from earlier versions of MS-DOS because they are unreliable. If you want to carry out backups from MS-DOS commands, use the MSBACKUP set rather then MWBACKUP.

Configuring MWBACKUP

MWBACKUP will not work right away, because it needs to be configured for your computer. This involves making a one-off trial backup and reading it back. You will need to have some floppy discs formatted ready for use. What this test does is to backup some test files onto a couple of floppies, and test that they can be read back with perfect accuracy. You will be asked to re-insert the discs in order.

Start by double-clicking on the MWBACKUP icon. You will see the notice about configuration appear (unless you have used the backup system before). Accept configuration if it is offered. You might need to remove any disc from the A: drive while it is being tested. You will then see a notice about using the A: drive for a trial backup. Click on the *Start* button when you are ready.

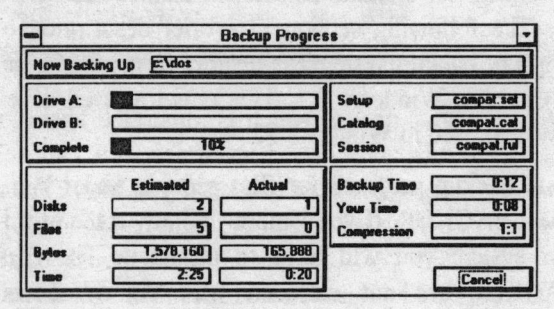

You will see a report on the screen, illustrated here, while the test is in progress. You will be asked to change discs at some stage. The second phase in configuration is reading back the backed up files from the floppy discs to check that they are perfect copies.

Floppy backup

When the screen notice about reading back the files appears, insert the first backup floppy in the drive and click on the OK button. You will see a progress report on the screen, and be told when to insert the second disc. When the comparison is finished, you will see a notice that the system is OK for using BACKUP.

If anything has gone wrong you will see messages to tell you. You should not attempt to use MWBACKUP until a compatibility test has reported success. If all is well you will see the main BACKUP menu, with the *Configure* item highlighted.

Making a Windows 3.1 backup

Start by clicking on the *Backup* icon in the *Backup* menu. You will see the panel change so that you can select the hard drive as the source of backups and the floppy drive as the destination. Now click on the *Select Files* button. There will be a pause while your directories are checked.

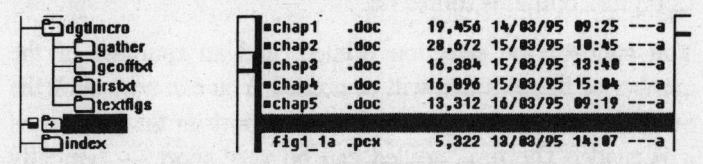

```
├─dgtlmcro          ■chap1   .doc    19,456  14/03/95  09:25  ---a
│  ├─gather         ■chap2   .doc    28,672  15/03/95  10:45  ---a
│  ├─gcoffbxt       ■chap3   .doc    16,384  15/03/95  13:40  ---a
│  ├─irsbxt         ■chap4   .doc    16,896  15/03/95  15:04  ---a
│  └─textflgs       ■chap5   .doc    13,312  16/03/95  09:19  ---a
├─□
└─□index           fig1_1a  .pcx     5,322  13/03/95  14:07  ---a
```

You will see a list, part of which is illustrated above, rather like your File Manager list, from which you can select a directory and files (more than one set if you like). You select a filename by clicking on it with the right-hand mouse button or using the Shift key and the left-hand mouse button. A square dot appears against selected files. You can de-select in the same way. A filename that has once been selected appears in red even when it has been deselected.

You can also select files by dragging the mouse with the right-hand mouse button held down, or you can specify a

Essentials of computer security

wildcard name in the *Include/Exclude* box, see illustration above. This can be done **only** if you first clear all selections by dragging the mouse with both buttons held down, altering the filenames from red to black. This takes effect only on the next backup when the Setup file (see later) is loaded.

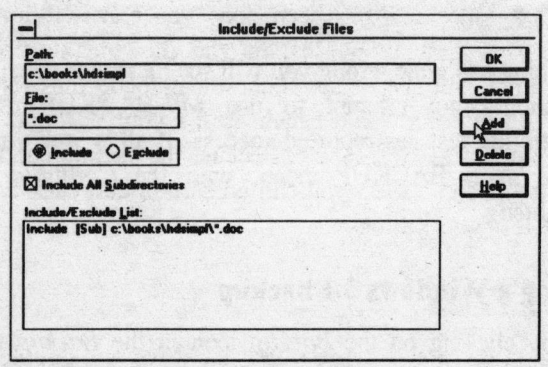

```
┌─────────────────────────────────────────────────┐
│ —              Include/Exclude Files            │
│ Path:                                    ┌────┐ │
│ c:\books\hdsimpl                         │ OK │ │
│                                          └────┘ │
│ File:                                   ┌──────┐│
│ *.doc                                   │Cancel││
│                                         └──────┘│
│  ● Include   ○ Exclude                  ┌────┐  │
│                                         │ Add│  │
│  ☒ Include All Subdirectories           └────┘  │
│                                         ┌──────┐│
│ Include/Exclude List:                   │Delete││
│ Include [Sub] c:\books\hdsimpl\*.doc    └──────┘│
│                                          ┌────┐ │
│                                          │Help│ │
│                                          └────┘ │
└─────────────────────────────────────────────────┘
```

Click on the *Add* button to add in your selection. You can add other file types, Include or Exclude files and change directory as required. Click the Options button and ensure that the Compress option is turned on.

You can see the selection printed, and an estimate of the number of floppies that will be needed. You can now click the Start Backup button. You will see a report on the backup as it is made. The time needed can be very short — typically about 3 seconds for the example of five document files totalling about 94 Kbyte. The compression factor can be as high as 4:1.

One of the very valuable features of MWBACKUP is that you can retain the options that you have made in the form of a file called a backup catalogue. For example, if you chose to backup all *.DOC files in a directory called C:\BOOKS\HDSIMPL, with compression, you can save these options as a catalogue file, with the SET extension.

Floppy backup

If you click the *File* option of Backup and then click on *Save Setup* you will save your setup as a file called DEFAULT.SET. All *Include* and *Exclude* options that you have made will then apply. If you want to use your own filename you can select *Save Setup As* and type the filename as needed. Once this has been done you can in future use Backup very quickly by loading the file and starting the backup. You can keep a set of these catalogue files for each type of backup you make, such as for your accounts files, your word-processor files, etc. Because the backup conditions are stored in these files, you can be certain that each backup will use the same options.

Restoring files

Place the first of the floppies into the drive and double-click on the MWBACKUP icon, so that the main menu appears. Click on the Restore icon. The menu that appears allows you to restore to the original directory or directories or the other drives or directories as illustrated here.

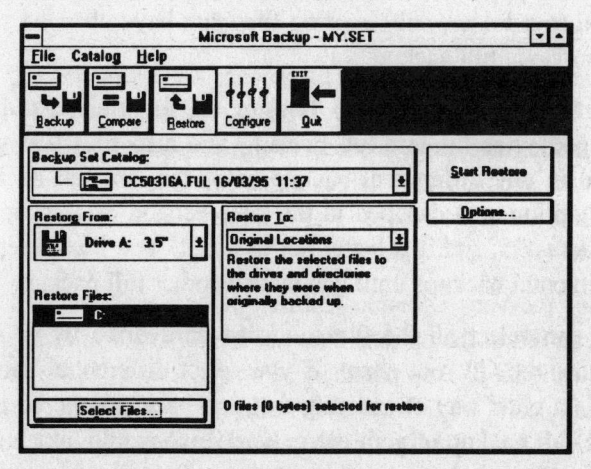

You can then use the *Select Files* button to see the files that have been backed up, and you can select which files you want

Essentials of computer security

to restore. Once you have selected files you can click *on Start Restore*. The action is very fast.

You can use the *Options* button to make choices about the Backup routines

MWBACKUP can carry out three forms of backup, called *Full, Incremental* and *Differential*. For most purposes you should use the *Full* backup. You should **always** use a Full backup for files that have never been backed up before. Thereafter you can use incremental or differential backup to keep track of changes.

You should, however, make another *Full* backup at intervals, typically of one week or one month, depending on how intensively you create and alter files.

An incremental backup will back up only the files that have changed since the last *Full* or *Incremental* backup. This is the most useful type of backup for general purposes, particularly if you edit a set of the same files each working day. An incremental backup will not include files that have been added to a folder, only existing files that have changed since the previous full backup.

A differential backup will backup all the files that have changed since the last full backup, and also files that were saved in any differential backup since the last full backup. This option was dropped in the later version of Backup for Windows 95, and it is better not to use it. You must keep all incremental backups until you make another full backup.

You can select all the files on your hard drive by double-clicking the C:\ root name. If you select differential backup this is a good way of ensuring that you back up altered files, but a full backup of your entire hard drive would take a long time and use a large number of discs. For example, a hard drive containing a modest 178 Mbyte would need 91 floppies

Floppy backup

and 76 minutes for backup. This is just an estimate, more might be needed — though if you use compression you will normally need fewer floppies than this report calls for. Now that most machines come with a hard drive size of 1 Gbyte or more, backup on floppies for the entire contents of a hard drive is simply not practicable.

This means that any backup using floppies has to be a selective backup of data rather than a backup of the whole drive. You must, however, keep one backup of the system files Because such a backup allows the disc directory structure to be restored as well as the files, it can be very useful if a portion of a disc becomes wiped or unusable.

4 Tape and other backups

Floppies can be used for backing up purposes provided that the amount of data that is to be backed up is relatively small. By the time that making a backup involves juggling with ten or more floppies, you need to start seriously considering other forms of backup. Some of these alternatives are now very much lower in price than they were just a few years ago, notably tape drives and external hard drives, so that if you once considered these backup methods and rejected them because of cost, now is the time to think again.

The main benefit of these other systems is that they allow a much greater amount of data to be recorded on one unit (tape or disc) than is possible when you use the conventional type of floppy. Against that consideration, their use means another device plugged into the computer, and another type of storage device (such as tape cartridges) that you have to buy. Another point is that you have to make allowance for growth in your requirements. You might need to back up just a few hundred Mbyte now, but what will you need in a few years time? Will the system you select be able to cope if you need more and more storage?

Note: Prices that are quoted in this and other chapters are manufacturer's prices with VAT included. Lower prices can usually be found by careful shopping. Many suppliers quote prices without VAT, a few show both prices.

High-capacity floppies

There are several types of drives that are classed as high-capacity floppies. These are based on the principle of either a much more precise guidance system for the magnetic read/write head than the conventional track and sector scheme can offer, or the use of a head that virtually floats on the surface of the magnetic coating. This, together with a suitable

Tape and other backups

magnetic coating on the disc, provides for about 100 Mbyte to be stored on what looks like any ordinary floppy.

The most familiar brand for this latter type of drive is IOmega, whose Zip drive is sometimes found fitted to new machines and which can be installed on an existing machine either internally or externally. The advantage of using such drives is that the disc is removable, like the normal 3½" disc, and that these discs can be interchanged between users, provided both users have the IOmega Zip drive.

The Zip drive can be installed externally and connected from a parallel port, or it can be internally fitted. If the internal fitting is used, it requires a SCSI type of interface card, and a suitable interface is supplied with the kit — a typical price is £175 including VAT. If you already use the SCSI interface for other drives you will not need to use the supplied card — but you do need to know how to configure SCSI drives and supply the correct ID number for the Zip drive. Most PC machines are fitted with the IDE or EIDE type of drives rather than the SCSI type.

If you are using Windows 95 the Zip drive can be used without any additional software, because Windows 95 is able to recognise SCSI devices when the hardware is present. Users of Windows 3.1 will need to use the operating software that is supplied. Operating software will normally provide the option of saving data in plain form or compressed. You would normally opt for the compressed form to achieve the maximum capacity of the disc or tape.

The Zip disc is, despite its appearance, not interchangeable with the conventional 3½" type, and each disc costs around £16.50, and holds 100 Mbyte without compression. Speed of use is faster than a conventional floppy or a tape drive, but noticeably slower than a hard drive.

Essentials of computer security

The Zip principle (a *Bernoulli* drive) has been around for some time, and several attempts have been made in the past to use a different method of obtaining more data on a 3½" floppy type of disc. Laser guidance systems have been tried, and in the past, one drive has been offered that allowed the use either of conventional floppies or of 21 Mbyte floppies interchangeably. Though this technology is still being considered, the fast development of optical drives is overtaking it so rapidly that it may not appear on the market.

External hard drives

The use of an external hard drive is one method that has gained in popularity as hard drive prices have fallen. External in this sense means that the drive is in a case of its own, not installed inside the casing of the computer, and is connected to the computer by way of a parallel port. This can be the printer port, if the printer cable is disconnected, or you can add another parallel port to your computer. Since the price of a parallel port card is very low and its installation is easy, this is preferable to disturbing the printer cable each time you want to make a backup.

External hard drive units can be obtained either as fixed hard drives or removable hard drives. The removable type is more satisfactory if you might in future need more capacity, because the same external unit can have different disc cartridges plugged into it.

The advantage of the external hard drive type of unit is that it is fast, not too expensive, and can provide for large amounts of data, particularly when used along with data compression. Suitable software will have to be provided by the manufacturers to allow the external hard drive to be allocated a drive letter and be recognised as one of the computer's removable drives. Once this has run, Microsoft Backup can

Tape and other backups

be used to place backup data on to the external drive as required.

There are several manufacturers of removable hard drive units, and the most recent example is the IOmega Jaz drive. This uses a 1 Gbyte hard drive cartridge, costing around £105, and the drive itself is priced at £587 for the external unit and £468 for the internal version. Connection for either version is by a SCSI card which is not supplied — you need to have a suitable card in your computer, which means that you must either be using a computer designed as a network server, or have fitted the SCSI card for yourself in place of the more usual IDE system. IOmega are likely to bring out new drives that can handle larger capacity cartridges, but it is fairly certain that the older type of cartridge can be read by the later drives.

QIC tape

The letters QIC mean *quarter-inch tape*, and refer to the type of tape cartridge that, until recently, was the standard for backing up data in amounts up to 350 Mbyte (compressed). The cartridge looks and feels nothing like a conventional tape cassette; it is made from metal, precisely built, heavy, and with no visible way of moving the tape. This is typical of data cassettes, and the system is very reliable and the cartridges very rugged.

The best-known of the QIC systems is the Colorado Jumbo (a Hewlett-Packard product), now obtainable at very low prices because commercial users now require much higher capacities. The *Backup* system of Windows 95 allows the use of built-in QIC 40, 80 and 3010 units, manufactured by Colorado, Conner, IOmega or Wangtek; or the externally connected parallel-port QIC types manufactured by Colorado. Other drives are not recognised, and must use their

Essentials of computer security

own software – this applies, for example, to the popular Travan type of drive (see later). Most of these units can be connected to the computer by way of existing controllers and cables; other systems often require a SCSI connection which is likely to be found only on large network server machines.

These QIC units can be bought as internal or external units. The internal type can be installed in a spare 5¼" bay, as used for the older type of floppy drive, and the external units can be placed next to the computer and connected by way of a parallel port. As noted earlier, it is much more convenient to fit an additional parallel port for these units rather than unplugging the printer connector.

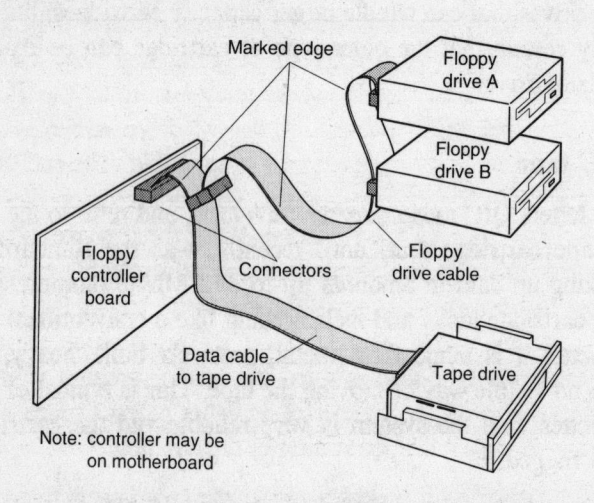

The method of installing an internal Colorado unit is described here because the installation of other tape backup units follows much the same pattern. Some installation manuals were written well before Windows 95 became available, so that you might have to exercise some discretion about software requirements if you are installing an older design of tape backup. The basis of the installation is that the tape drive is connected by way of the floppy drive connection

Tape and other backups

within the computer, as illustrated. This is done using an adapter cable so that if you are already using two floppy drives you can continue to do so if there is space in the computer for another drive.

If you need to remove a floppy drive B: to provide space to install a tape unit, you will need to alter the computer's CMOS RAM settings to show that no B: drive is installed. Consult the manual for your computer to find out how to alter the CMOS RAM settings to show that no B: drive is fitted. No changes are needed in the CMOS RAM settings to allow for the added tape drive.

With the computer switched off and the case opened, you will need to install the data cable. Some types of drive may allow the second floppy connector to be used, but the Colorado requires an adapter cable to be plugged in to the floppy controller board. The existing floppy drive cable is then plugged into a connector on this adapter cable. The end of the adapter cable is then plugged into the connector on the tape drive. Care must be taken when making these connections to keep the coloured identification stripe on the cable facing to the correct end of the connector. This stripe shows the side of the connector that houses pin 1. All of this is much easier to do before the tape unit is fixed into place, because it is not easy to see when the connector is in its correct place when you are peering round the casing of the computer.

Once the connection has been made, the tape unit is fixed into the brackets for the floppy drive B. The conventional 5¼" drive bay must be used — modern computers usually provide a generous number of these bays as well as the conventional 3½" bay. The tape unit is fixed using the screws that are provided — these are either 6-32 UNC × 0.31 ($^5/_{16}$") or metric M 40.7-6H. You might find that the frame of the drive is stamped M for metric or S for UNC. If you lose these

Essentials of computer security

screws or if they are not supplied you must not on any account attempt to use other screws even if they appear to be of the correct size, and you must not try to drill other fixing holes. UNC bolts are not easy to find, but electronics suppliers such as Maplin can supply the metric types.

When the tape unit is bolted into place, the power connector can be plugged in. This is shaped so that it will fit only one way round, with the bevelled edge uppermost, and modern computers provide a generous number of power connectors so that there should be no difficulty in finding one that will reach the tape unit, as illustrated here.

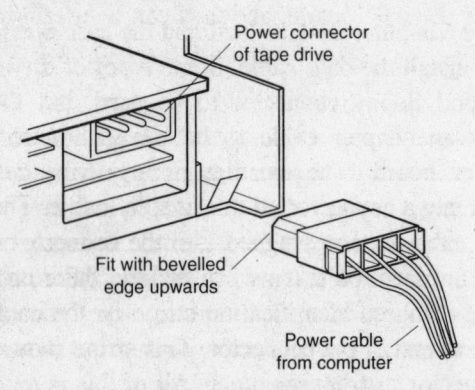

Once the unit is physically installed, you can close up the casing again and start up the computer. The tape drive will not be recognised until an installation program is run, and this usually involved putting a supplied floppy into the floppy drive and running a SETUP program. Once this program has run, you should be able to start Microsoft Backup (a program which was written in conjunction with Colorado) and see the icon for a tape backup unit appear among your other drives.

Once the unit is working, its use follows the pattern that was described in detail in Chapter 3, except that the tape drive is selected for backup, restore and compare, rather than floppies. The Jumbo type of drive allow you to use tapes of

Tape and other backups

the DC2120 type, and these can be obtained unformatted or formatted. If time is important to you, the extra price of the formatted type saves time in formatting. With compression switched on (as is the default) the DC2120 will provide the equivalent of 250 Mbyte of storage, and the longer DC2120XL tape will provide 350 Mbyte. Tape prices range between £7 and £12.

During backup actions, log files are created. These are called Error.log and are located in the Program Files — Accessories — Log folder, which is normally placed on the C:\ drive. These log files hold details of what has happened in a backup, restore or compare action, and they can be useful in the event of a failure. You do not normally need to keep all log files, only the most recent.

The separate Colorado software allows for restoring the contents of a hard drive after a catastrophic failure which has required replacement of the drive. This uses a System (*Startup*) floppy disc with the Colorado software on it. There is no provision for this action in the Microsoft Backup version, but if you use the Colorado drive, you can prepare floppies for this type of emergency, but use Microsoft Backup for your normal backup actions.

Other tape cartridges

A number of tape systems of higher capacity have been evolved since the Colorado Jumbo types. Colorado can now supply the Travan tape units, some of which are compatible with the DC2120 types, but which can also use a cartridge capable of much greater capacity. At the time of writing, the older Travan T1000 model allows the use of DC2120 or T1000 (TR1) cartridges, and the T1000 cartridge will store up to 800 Mbyte. The more recent Travan T4000S is not

Essentials of computer security

compatible with the DC2120 tapes of the older machines, and uses a T4 cartridge storing up to 8Gbyte.

Between these extremes you can buy tape drives of a range of capacities, using cartridges that range in price between about £8 and £30. For home users, the lowest-priced Jumbo unit is probably adequate — remember that you do not need to back up all of your data onto one single tape. For example, it is often better to make one system backup tape which contains all of Windows 95 and associated files, and use other tapes for other programs and for data. By splitting up your requirements, you can work with 1Gbyte or more of backup data in a drive that handles only 350 Mbyte cartridges. Note that the figure of 350 Mbyte applies to compressed files only — if you opt not to use compression the file capacity will be much lower.

DAT and similar units

The Colorado T4000S and Connor TSM-4000 can backup data to the tune of several Gbytes, but for commercial users faster action and greater capacity (if needed) can be obtained using DAT (digital audio tape) units. As the name suggests, these units use the mechanisms that were developed for 8 mm digital cassettes for audio.

The DAT system was available in the Far East several years ago, but its release in Europe was delayed because of the worries of record manufacturers about copying from CDs, since digital systems can make perfect copies even when serial copying is used (meaning making a copy of a copy of a copy...). Modern audio DAT units bought in the UK use software that prevents more than one copy being made of a CD.

For computer backup purposes single DAT units, usually of 2 Gbyte to 4 Gbyte capacity can be installed internally using

Tape and other backups

a 5¼" bay, but they are also available in stacks allowing total capacities of up to 64 Gbyte. Unlike the simpler tape units, these connect to the computer using the SCSI type of interface. It is unlikely that any computer requiring this amount of backup would not already use SCSI interfaces.

The DAT drive uses a rotating head construction which is identical in principle to the system used for video-cassette recorders (VCRs), and a VCR can also provide an excellent low-cost mechanism for backup. All that is required is an interface board, suitable software and suitable connecting cables, and your old VCR, discarded perhaps when you buy a more recent model, can become your backup system.

The advantages are comparatively cheap hardware, the main part of which is the VCR that you might already possess, very cheap tapes (much cheaper than the cheapest of QIC cartridges, for example) and very large capacity (several Gbytes) on a standard E180 tape. The only snag is the size of the VCR.

Given these advantages, you might imagine that every retailer would be stocking the adapter kit, but the drawback is that this type of system does not appeal to commercial users, and has been aimed only at the hobby user of backup. Since hobby users do not normally require much in the way of backup, only a few small advertisements have appeared, and I have not printed the address here in case the supplier has vanished by the time this book goes to press. If this type of system appeals to you, I can only recommend that you keep an eye on advertisements in the magazines.

Optical units

Optical storage, such as is used for CD-ROM is yet another way of providing quite large capacities for backup, though not as high as some modern cartridge, DAT or VCR systems.

Essentials of computer security

Optical storage comes in two main varieties. The ROM type uses the same principles as CD-ROM, and though at one time the equipment needed for recording on the familiar silver disc was very high, the price has now fallen to be comparable with that of a DAT unit.

The other variety is in many way more interesting, and one predominant type at the time of writing is strictly speaking classed as magneto-optical storage. Without going into details, it uses a laser beam to alter the magnetism of a film of material, and the changes in magnetism can be used on readout to alter a reading laser beam and so provide digital signals. A disc can be re-written several thousand times without deterioration, and the storage is permanent unless another writing action is performed — the magnetism is much more permanent than that of a floppy. The significance of using a laser beam is that it can be focused to a very small point, much smaller than any conventional magnetic pickup head could be made.

There is another technology, also based on laser beams and called the phase-change drive. These drives, developed by Panasonic, use the heating effect of the laser to alter the surface of the disc, and claim to allow at least 500,000 re-recording actions without deterioration. Another advantage is that these drives can be used as conventional CD-ROM players as well as being re-recordable drives. All of the 'silver disc' systems claim that the discs will have a life of at least 30 years.

Using the CD-ROM system allows you to make backups which are more permanent than a conventional magnetic recording, with all the immunity to rough treatment that a conventional CD possesses. These are, however, ROMs in the sense that once created they cannot be altered or re-written, so they are mainly for archival purposes where precious data has to be preserved for long periods. If the data

Tape and other backups

changes, another disc has to be created for the new data, but at prices of around £5 for a blank disc this is cheaper than tape backup.

The magneto-optical discs are available in two sizes at present. The smaller type is about the size of a 3½" floppy, and will store up to 230 Mbyte. The larger discs can store up to 1.3 Gbyte, and one type allows both sides to be used, giving a total capacity of 2.6 Gbyte.

One of the first magneto-optical drives to become well established was the Fujitsu, which uses the smaller type of disc storing up to 230 Mbyte. The drive can be obtained in internal or external versions, and uses the SCSI type of connection, with a suitable card included so that you can use this drive even if your computer uses the more usual EIDE system. The drive price is £468 and the disc price is given as £23.50, making this system relatively expensive for the amount of data that can be saved. Against this, the small disc is convenient and useful for data interchange between users.

At the other end of the magneto-optical scale, Plasmon supplies an external drive that uses large discs with the provision for using both sides to give a total capacity of 2.6 Gbyte. This is an external drive of the SCSI variety, so that you need to be using a computer with an existing SCSI card and suitable software (either Windows 95 or other SCSI driver software). At a drive cost of £2,732 and disc cost of £87 this unit is not intended for the small-scale user, but it is ideal for the commercial user with large amounts of data to store or transfer.

At the time of writing, all of the phase-change drives make use of the Panasonic mechanism in external cases connected through the SCSI card. Panasonic's own drive comes complete with a suitable SCSI card and cable at a price of around £527, with disc cost of £38. As usual, if you are

Essentials of computer security

running Windows 95 (or Windows NT) no additional drivers will be needed, but two drive letters will be assigned, one for reading CD-ROM and the other for the read-write discs. The maximum storage capacity is 640 Mbyte, as for CD-ROM.

Testing

Whatever backup system is in use, it is very important to carry out thorough testing. After all, if you are entrusting all of your data to a cartridge or a disc, you do not want to find out how to recover data when your livelihood depends on it, and you certainly don't want to leave it until that moment to find that your backup system does not work.

Carrying out a comparison action is one way of soothing the nerves. If you have just saved data and you use the *Compare* action before the data on the hard drive is changed, you should get a message to the effect that the backed-up data is identical to the data on the hard drive. This is a considerable comfort, but it is not enough to ensure total peace of mind. You can be totally sure of your system only when:

- You have recovered files from it
- You have checked backups regularly over a long period
- You have restored your data after a hard-drive crash.

Of these, the last is the most difficult to achieve. No-one wants to spend the time and take the risk of erasing all the contents of a hard drive just to make sure that the backup system works, and alternative methods, noted below, are costly. Nevertheless, you cannot be utterly certain that your business would survive such a catastrophe unless you have rehearsed it, though you can be reasonably confident if the system has allowed you to recover archived files at intervals.

Tape and other backups

If you have more than one computer with a backup system, you might try out backup on a computer whose hard drive information was also backed up on another hard drive on another computer. You could then delete the contents of that hard drive without having to worry quite so much about recovery. Another possibility is to fit a new hard drive as a second hard drive on a computer, and see if you can restore the whole of a system and its data files to the new drive. This is a particularly useful test, because it checks out much of what you will need to do in the event of a hard drive becoming unusable. It is also a very useful way of preparing a new hard drive to take over the actions of an older drive that is about to be retired.

All such testing takes time, and if you feel that a complete restoration test is more than you want to try, then make sure that you do at least **know** how to do it. Remember that when a hard drive fails, you will need to be able to start (boot) the computer from a floppy, but such a floppy (called a startup disc) will **not** allow you to run Windows. You must therefore know how to carry out the restoration of your system (Windows 95 and all that goes with it) and data files by using only the bare MS-DOS commands that such a floppy permits. This is always more difficult than the use of the backup for normal files, and you should keep several copies of clear step-by-step instructions in places where you can get to them in an emergency. By all means keep one copy near the computer, but have another one, and preferably several, in a much safer place.

The best practice is to make sure that you never need a complete restoration. If you change computers to keep up to date with technology, you are unlikely to wear out a hard drive. If you do not change computers at reasonably short intervals (such as every three years), make sure that you check the condition of the main hard drive at intervals, and

Essentials of computer security

watch for signs of imminent failure. Replacing a hard drive before it fails is by far the least stressful way of keeping your data secure, particularly since you can install the new drive in the machine along with the old one until all of the files have been copied over. Another useful tip is to spread your data over several hard drives. Some very large network server machines use the RAID (redundant array of independent discs) system to make sure that data is automatically stored in duplicate on more than one hard drive.

5 Keeping backups safe

Making backups is one thing, keeping them safe is quite another. Making a backup certainly allows you to recover your software in the event of a hard drive crash, but you need to do more to protect against theft or damage from fire or flood. A complete or partial backup might consist of a set of floppies, one or more tape cartridges, perhaps a hard drive cartridge or an optical disc. Whatever hazards apply to your computer now apply equally to the backups, and you need to give as much consideration to where and how they are stored as to making them in the first place.

Remember that these backups are valuable. The computer is only a piece of machinery that can be insured, but the backups contain all the data that is confidential to you, and if the data on the computer is worth anything to other people, then the data on the backups is also. It might certainly be compressed so that it needs Microsoft Backup to read it, but anyone who steals backups will certainly have the ability to read them. Your backups must therefore be in as physically safe a place as your computer, and preferably something better.

Short-term security is often neglected. Once you have made backups, don't let the discs or tapes sit beside the computer. Even if the only immediate place for them is your pocket, that's better than leaving them where they are. If you are called away from the computer or from the office for only a moment, take your backups with you or put them in a secure place. For the short term, this need not be a safe or strong-room, only a place where an opportunist thief would not look unless he/she had considerable time to spare.

Essentials of computer security

Long-term storage

The long-term storage of backups requires more care and thought than short-term care. To start with, there are several different classes of long term storage, such as:

- Archival storage of backups that might be kept for many years
- Precautionary storage of backups in case of a hard-drive failure
- Storage as a precaution against fire, flood or theft.

Archival storage is needed for records that would be too bulky to store in paper form but which are not likely to be needed for many years. At present, most users of archival storage (such as solicitors) still use paper alone, but the increasing use of scanners and optical backup now makes it possible to store in much more compact forms. At one time, the mistrust of digital storage was based on the unreliability of magnetic recording in the 1960s, but things have moved on, and the commercial world will eventually catch up.

Archival storage on paper is just as much at risk from fire, flood and theft as data storage on any form of backup, and the main issue as far as data storage is concerned is how long magnetic backups can be held. The durability of tape backups is reasonably well known, because digitally recorded tape has been in use now for several decades.

Nevertheless, optical recording is, in many ways, more suited for archival backup. Though tape may be as enduring as paper, the magnetic signals on it are more vulnerable. You can check the contents of paper archives at intervals to make sure that the print is not fading and that they are not being eaten by mice or termites, but invisible magnetic signals on tape or disc are not so easy to check. By contrast, purely

Keeping backups safe

optical discs are unaffected by magnetism, and even the magneto-optical type are unaffected by magnetic fields of any size that would occur outside a research laboratory.

One considerable attraction of optical data backups for archival use is that making multiple copies is almost as cheap and easy as making one copy, so that there is no need to have all of your precious eggs in one dubious basket. This is a considerable advantage compared to paper storage, and one that must weight heavily on the side of this type of backup for archives. It is likely that users of archival backup, such as solicitors, will want to keep original papers only because they can be shown to clients, with the real backup in the form of optical discs.

Storage for archival backup needs to be carefully thought out, and the criteria for storage space are that it must be safe from fire, flood, theft and, if magnetic media are stored, violent changes in magnetic fields. Since all of these except magnetic protection are the criteria for the storage of banknotes and valuable documents, the obvious places to store your archival backups are in a bank vault or with a solicitor who can offer similar security.

On a smaller scale, you may be able to provide vault-like security for yourself. In these days of plastics and sealing methods it is not difficult to place backups into a container that is sealed against water, and bury the container in a safe place to protect it against fire or theft. The main proviso here is that it can be retrieved again, because archival storage means periods of thirty years or more, and if you or your successors want to retrieve the data and find that it is buried in a piece of ground that has now become a motorway or a high-rise block, your storage scheme will not seem such a good idea.

Essentials of computer security

Precautionary long-term backup against hard drive failure is mainly concerned with what is needed to get running again after such a failure. The data on the hard drive will probably have been backed up separately, usually a short-term backup if the data is changing and being backed up each week. This leaves the requirement of keeping backups of the operating system and programs, and even these will change at intervals.

This form of backup, then, need not be concerned with such long time periods as archival backup, and you might want to renew the backups annually, half-yearly, perhaps even quarterly. The storage system is also less crucial because all of your programs, could, if it came to the crunch, be restored from their original distribution discs or new copies could be bought. Obviously, the backups should not be stored in the same place as these original distribution discs. A safe, a cellar, a locked room are reasonable resting places for such backups, and because backups are not bulky they are reasonably easy to hide in such spaces.

Storage against the hazards of fire, flood and theft is mainly applicable to data which, unlike programs, cannot be replaced and which is notoriously difficult to insure. Because we are talking here about data which is frequently being changed rather than archival data, the main concern is short-term storage, and though this should be in a secure place if your data must not be seen by others, it has to be a place which is accessible to anyone who needs to use the backups.

The proven best method for such backups is the grandfather, father, son system as was mentioned in Chapter 1. By far the best way of dealing with storage is to distribute the copies, so that no single storage place contains more than one copy. For example, you might keep the son copy in a locked office, the father copy in a safe place at home, and the grandfather copy in your pocket. Even this scheme could be tedious if data is

Keeping backups safe

backed up daily, but the principle of distributing copies is a sound one.

Distributing copies

The added security that comes from distributing copies of backups applies even more strongly to backups that need to be held for longer periods. The snag is that distributed copies are more vulnerable to theft, but if what is backed up cannot be used to blackmail you, ruin your business, or get you sued, then theft is less of a worry, because it is most unlikely that all the copies would be stolen. It is equally unlikely that all of the copies would suffer loss from fire or flood, so that the security of the data is good.

The security advantages of distributing copies exist only if the distribution is reasonably wide. It would, for example, be pointless to place copies into three offices in the same block, because all copies would then be at the same risk. If the copies are at three quite different addresses they are much more secure because there is no reason to expect an event at one address to affect the others.

Distribution need not be at fixed places. Carrying one copy in your car and keeping one at home can provide some security, though at least one backup of the full operating system should be kept in a bank vault, particularly when you are on holiday or abroad. As long as the principle of spreading the risk is kept in mind, distribution can greatly increase this type of security.

Backup computers

If you depend on one single computer for your livelihood, consider using a backup computer for security. This need not be as extravagant as it sounds. For the past decade or so, the average working life of a computer has been three years or

Essentials of computer security

less because of the relentless technical progress in both hardware and software, chasing ever higher speeds and larger memory size.

At some stage, you will upgrade your computer to something faster and with larger capacity, and since the old machine has little or no trade-in value, consider keeping it, particularly if it is equipped with the same backup system as the new machine. The old machine can then be kept in safer place, less liable to be stolen and preferably at less risk from the other hazards.

In the event of loss of the new machine, the backups can be used on the old one. You might have to suffer some loss of speed, perhaps be unable to juggle with as many programs at a time, perhaps unable to deal with all of the data on the hard drive at the same time, but at least you can keep going. If your business depends on deadlines, as so many do in the age of 'just in time', keeping going is essential, and the spare machine is a lifeline.

Another variation on this theme is to have a spare backup drive which can be installed into any PC if required, so that you can borrow a machine or even buy one off the shelf, install the drive and make use of your backups. The principle is the same, to get back to work as soon as possible after the loss of a computer. If your work requires Email or other communications you might want to keep an older model of modem as a spare as well.

Erasure

What happens when you delete a file or a directory? Its name vanishes from the directory display, and the display of available disc space rises so that you can with confidence save more files in that space. In fact, only the name is really deleted, and the bytes of the file remain on place on the disc. All that has really happened is that the portion of the disc that

Keeping backups safe

your file occupied now carries a sign advertising that it is available for other use. Until another file is saved and takes up the space, the bytes of your 'deleted' file are still in place.

Because the bytes of the file are still on the disc, any file can be un-deleted. At one time this was a highly-skilled action that needed considerable knowledge of MS-DOS and a fair amount of experience.

Nowadays it's a lot easier using the *Recycle Bin* of Windows 95. When you 'delete' a file from Windows 95, the only effect is to shift the file to another folder, the Recycle Bin. The file is totally unaffected, simply removed from its current position, and it is not deleted when another file is saved, even if the new file uses the same filename.

If you realise that you have deleted a file in error, it is easy to retrieve it. Simply open the *Recycle Bin* folder (which is on the Desktop, or in the Windows Explorer display), select your file or files and click *Restore* from the *File* menu. This will restore the file to its original position, but if you use the Explorer display, you can simply copy or move the file from the Recycle Bin to another folder.

When a file is deleted under Windows 95, no more space is made available on the hard drive until the Recycle Bin is emptied (from the File menu when the Recycle Bin folder is selected in Windows Explorer or from the Desktop). This action makes the disc space available for reuse, so that the file will become totally impossible to recover once new files have been saved.

You can click the *Properties* item on the *File* menu when the Recycle Bin is selected in Windows Explorer. This brings up a panel labelled *Global*, with options for your drive(s). If you use more than one hard drive (which can include each partition of a partitioned drive), you can opt to configure each drive separately, so that each drive has its own bin. The

Essentials of computer security

option is to use global settings for all hard drives. If you opt to configure separately, the panel will have labelled tabs for each separate drive letter, as shown here.

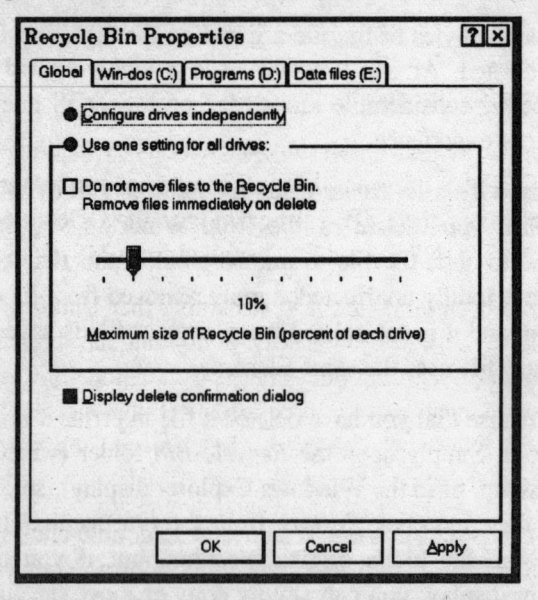

```
Recycle Bin Properties                              [?][X]
Global | Win-dos (C:) | Programs (D:) | Data files (E:)
       ● Configure drives independently
       ● Use one setting for all drives:
         ☐ Do not move files to the Recycle Bin.
           Remove files immediately on delete

         |----------|----------|
                   10%
         Maximum size of Recycle Bin (percent of each drive)

         ■ Display delete confirmation dialog

                    OK    Cancel    Apply
```

There is another option to avoid the use of the Recycle Bin, and remove files from folder display immediately they are deleted. This is an option that few users will require, because the Recycle Bin system is such a useful way of having second thoughts about what you delete — you can wait until you are certain that you do not need the deleted item.

Because items sent to the Recycle Bin are still stored, there is provision for fixing the maximum percentage of the hard drive that can be used for such 'deleted' files, so that you do not fill the hard drive. If you use more than one hard drive or drive letter, this percentage can be set to a different amount for each. It is set by dragging the pointer of the slide display left (less space) or right (more space). Typical values are from 2% to 10%.

Keeping backups safe

You can opt to display a delete confirmation warning and though this is not so necessary when you are using the Recycle Bin system it is essential if you opt to delete directly, and still useful even if you are using the Recycle Bin system.

Windows 3.1 undelete

Windows 3.1 can carry out undelete actions by making use of the MWUNDEL program that you should have in a Windows 3.1 group somewhere. This program is in the DOS directory, not in C:\WINDOWS, and it is installed from MS-DOS 6.22.

Before you even think about it, remember that Undelete has a good chance of succeeding only if nothing has been saved since the deletion action. There is a moderate chance otherwise, and absolutely none at all if the disc has been defragmented since the deletion. Undelete will tell you what the chances are of recovering a named file.

To use this program from Windows 3.1, double-click on the MWUNDEL icon from its group in Windows. You will see the MWUNDEL panel appear. By default this will show the C:\ directory, and any deleted files will appear in the display.

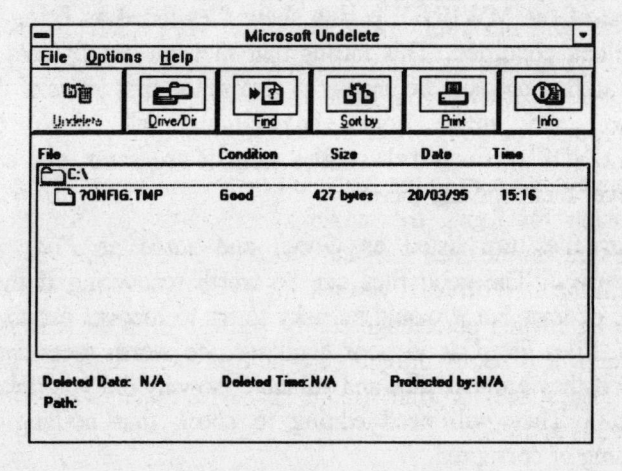

Essentials of computer security

The *Undelete* option will be greyed out until one or more file names are selected. You can use the *Drive/Dir* button to change to another drive or directory, and the *Find* option to look for files. You can also use the *Sort By* options to sort files into order of name, type date, etc.

The *File Condition* is also shown. If the file condition is shown as *Good* it is recoverable, but not necessarily totally intact. This is all right for a text file, but it would be distinctly dodgy if you were trying to recover, for example, a program file or an Excel workbook file.

When you click on the *Undelete* button you will be asked to type in the first letter of the selected file name and then click on the OK button.

You do not need to restore the identical character — any letter or number character will do if you have forgotten the old version. The only essential thing is to type in some letter. The missing first character is due to the way that a deleted file is indicated — the original character is replaced by an invisible code that is used by the computer to signal a file as deleted.

Some of the MWUNDEL lists show files listed as being in excellent condition. This means that they are totally intact, and all that needs to be done is to restore the first letter of the name, and make some calculations (all done by MWUNDEL). Even if these files were of programs, you can recover them and use them.

Other files are listed as *Good*, and some as *Poor* or *Destroyed*. The good files can be worth recovering if they were of text, but it would be risky to try to recover program files. Files listed as in poor condition are worth recovering only if they are text files and valuable (so why did you delete them?). They will need editing to check that nothing is missing or corrupted.

Keeping backups safe

MWUNDEL offers several levels of protection that you can set.

The *Standard* level of protection is useful and not difficult to work with — it only requires you to supply a first character for each filename, and that character need not be the original. A useful tip is always to use a character, such as Q, that would not appear in your filenames normally. This enables you to distinguish files that have been deleted and subsequently recovered from those which have not been deleted at any time.

The other two levels of Undeletion are called respectively *Tracker* and *Sentry*. Both require disc and memory space, but Tracker requires only a very small amount of disc space. Tracker works by keeping a small file of deleted files with their locations on the disc. This allows for quick and easy undeleting, but the files can still be corrupted by saving other files after deleting the old ones. Only the Sentry level of MWUNDEL can cope with this problem and allow complete recovery. The Sentry system is the nearest that Windows 3.1 gets to the Recycle Bin system of Windows 95.

The Sentry system operates by keeping a hidden directory that is used to hold deleted files. You can opt for what maximum number of files to hold or for how long files should be retained before being finally deleted (purged).

Sentry will hold files intact despite later file saving, but because your hard drive space is limited you must specify limits to what you retain in this way. Only files protected by Sentry are classed as *Perfect* by MWUNDEL and can **always** be recovered in perfect condition.

6 On-line security

Common worries

One very common worry that concerns computer users with important data is that the data may become available to a hacker who is at the end of a phone line, burrowing away undetected among the files. Despite the headlines that hacking gets, this sort of thing is much less common that you think, and most of the burrowing through your data is done by people who have immediate access to it.

Security for any computer that is put on line is important, and attention has to be paid to password use, and who has access to passwords. Undoubtedly hackers do sometimes gain access to privileged information, but not by some magical method that cannot be overcome. The most common failings are not protecting the data at all, or using a password that can be easily guessed by anyone who knows something about you.

Hackers are very seldom, if ever, people who are scanning the telephone numbers with the hope of finding something interesting. When a computer is hacked, it is nearly always by someone who has at some time worked in the same office and who has information, or someone with a close friend in that office.

For such a hacker, finding or guessing passwords is made infinitely easier, knowing that people tend to use passwords such as their date of birth, car registration numbers, wife/husband's name, and other such easily discoverable items. Using such passwords is the equivalent to leaving your car on the road with the keys inside and a guide to its security alarm neatly placed on the front seat.

Private users of computers are unlikely to suffer from hacking because they have a low profile. The most likely

On-line security

targets are commercial organisations who have at one time employed and later dismissed computer programmers (not necessarily people who were paid for programming as a full-time job). The hacker knows the telephone numbers to ring to make computer contact, is likely to know passwords, and also knows what information is likely to be of use.

Using passwords

Passwords can be a useful barrier against improper use of computer facilities, but only if the passwords are not known to anyone who is not entitled to them, and impossible to discover by guessing. If more than one person knows and uses a password, that password should be changed fairly frequently, and all passwords should be changed when people with computer knowledge (not necessarily professionals) are dismissed.

Despite the name, a password need not consist of letters only, and a password which is a combination of letters and digits is often harder to crack than one composed of letters alone. In addition, the greater the number of characters in the password, the more difficult it is to crack by any system of guessing. Six characters are often used, giving about 300,000,000 possible combination of letters, and this rises to 2,000,000,000 if digits 0 to 9 can also be used. These numbers are large enough to ensure that it would be difficult to find a password by systematically trying each combination (with the combinations generated by computer), but if one or two characters are known, the task becomes easier.

Some systems use very long and elaborate passwords. These are fine if they are used only once or twice, perhaps to validate a user's initial right on the system, but they become prohibitive if, for example, they have to be used each time access to a file is needed. Faced with such a password, the

Essentials of computer security

normal human reaction is to write it down, and that action enormously increases the security risks.

A good password should be reasonably short, easy for the user to remember, and unguessable by anyone else. That might seem an impossible combination of virtues, but there is a well-tried system that can produce such passwords.

What you need is a phrase you can always remember. It might be the first line of a song, the punchline of a joke, the last line of a poem. You then take the first letter of each word in the phrase, and make this your password. For example, if you remember 'Oh for the wings of a dove' this becomes OFTWOAD, which is not a word that is obvious to anyone who does not know how you have come by your password, and is not difficult for you to remember.

How to be immune from hackers

There is one simple way to be immune from all telephone hacking, and that's not to be on-line. If you have no modem connected to the telephone lines your computer cannot be connected to other computers over these lines, and no-one can possibly use the telephone system to hack into your files.

That is, of course, a perfect solution, but if the work that you do demands that you have to go on-line at times, it is an impossible solution. You can, however, work in a way that will make it very difficult for any hacker to get into your system.

Getting into your system, meaning being able to locate and read or alter files, from a remote site depends on suitable software running on your computer. If such software is not running, your computer cannot be hacked in this way, and many users of modems will possess, and not need to use, such software. If you need to use telephone networking, so that

On-line security

people in offices in other buildings can share your computer over the public telephone lines, then you are at risk, but only while this software is running.

The golden rule, then, is to allow this sharing on as restricted a basis as possible. Run the sharing system only when and as required, and dial up your other half immediately the software starts to run. Use some sort of passwording system to establish contact, and make this a password that is used from memory, not stored in the computer. Switch off the modem or the software if anything untoward seems to be happening.

The point here is that hacking is very unlikely to happen when you are actively using the computer, and the main risk is to computers that run unattended at night. Once again, the risk is greatest when software permits the outsider access to run programs, and if this is done very strict passwording needs to be enforced, because the computer must store the password.

Start a security review by asking a number of fundamental questions:

- Does this computer need to be connected to a modem at all?
- Does the modem need to be switched on at all times?
- What software exists — does it permit file sharing?
- Can this file sharing be supervised?
- Can programs be run by remote control?

By concentrating on what is needed, you can often reduce the risk by a very considerable extent, or even eliminate it.

The greatest problem exists when a large number of computers are networked together and the network server is on line. If you need to interchange information with other

Essentials of computer security

computers during the night, is there any possibility of using a computer which can be disconnected from the network, and which contains only the files that need to be shared? It is seldom necessary for all the machines on a network to be exposed to the same risk, and if the machine that is kept on-line is not the network server, it is possible to switch off the server and so isolate the rest of the network from the on-line machine.

Risks are much lower if a dedicated data line is used rather than a telephone line that can be dialled. Any hacking then requires tapping into that line, something that needs more effort, specialised knowledge and possibly assistance than the average hacker is likely to be able to call upon. Most large-scale users of data exchange will already have dedicated ISDN lines and any attempts to hack such lines will become a concern of the line owners, who have specialised knowledge, as well as the users.

Internal security.

As this and other chapters have suggested, the public image of a hacker as a spotty teenager who is trying telephone numbers at random to make contact with your computer, is a myth, and many reported incidents are blown up beyond belief. Given a level of security equivalent to locking your front door when you go out, the greatest risk to your data is not from hackers who do not know you from Adam, but from disgruntled employees or former employees.

These are people who know what they are looking for, know access numbers and possibly also passwords, and who may have a motive. These are people who can guess a simple password because they know your initials, your car registration number, the name of your dog and all the other words that so many users think will suffice as a password.

On-line security

Internal security is therefore of first importance, and only when this is in place need you start to worry about external phone users.

The first priority is to use passwords in a secure way. If you, and you alone, know a password, make it a secure one by using the scheme that has been suggested here — or anything else that results in a password that you can remember but which is gibberish to anyone else. Make sure that you do not write this password down or tell anyone else what it is. Make sure that no-one is looking over your shoulder when you use the password. This should ensure a good level of security.

'Should' is the operative word, but this depends on how well the password is stored in the computer. The computer software must contain a copy of your password in order to recognise it, and the security of a password very much depends on how easily it could be read from the computer. Not so long ago, it was quite common for a password to be kept in a file in clear form, in other words, not coded to make it unidentifiable. If you used the password QRCTZZX then at some place in the computer a file called, for example, PASSKEY would contain this word. This system assumed that any user of the computer would not know how to find this file and use it. Since these days, we have become a little less naive about people's knowledge of computers.

Nevertheless, the password needs to be stored, and currently it will be disguised somehow. One popular system is to shift by 13, meaning that each character is replaced by another, based on moving the position 13 places in the alphabet (taking A as the letter following Z). This has, however, become so well-known that it cannot be considered a safe method, particularly if it appears in a file called *Password* or in a line of a larger data file such as a Windows INI file.

Essentials of computer security

More elaborate systems use better ways of encrypting the password, so that no simple replacement of letters is used to make the coded version. Even this is not totally secure, however, because the program that accepts the password must contain a routine that decrypts it, and a user with inside knowledge of the program can obtain the password. This, however, restricts access to a comparatively small number of people with insider knowledge. Incidentally, this is much the same level of passwording as is used on the PIN number of a credit or debit card, because these numbers have to be encoded on to the magnetic stripe.

Security is most difficult to enforce when several users know a password. At least one of these users will probably write the password down, and this is more likely if the password is a good one which appears to be gibberish to anyone else. There is no simple solution, because even if you use the suggested method of a memorable phrase, it need not be memorable to anyone else, though if a user writes down the phrase it might not be quite so obvious as writing the password.

All that can be done is to urge careful use of passwords, and to change them at intervals. Passwords should certainly be changed if key staff are dismissed, particularly if the parting was not amicable (is it ever?). Even if the office is running smoothly, changing passwords at random intervals is a good precaution, because if a password has leaked it may be some time before anyone makes use of it.

Using the Internet and Email.

The Internet and Email are often cited as if they were an invitation to hackers. Unless you use Email to send everyone your passwords, there is no reason to worry unduly. Most Internet activities consist of reading documents or storing

On-line security

files on the hard drive, and these are not dangerous activities unless the document contain programs ('click on the icon to see what you get' messages for example). If you load in a program, or a document that contains a program (and this can include a Word or WordPerfect macro), there is a risk that running the program might activate a virus (see Chapter 7). The obvious remedy is to be choosy about your contacts. If you are reading material put on the net by an international organisation, there is little reason to worry — if you are certain that you know who you were in contact with.

If you have doubts, save programs on a floppy disc and run them on a computer which is not connected to the office network and does not contain any information of importance. If the program covers the screen with pointless images, messages from aliens, or wipes your hard drive you have at least avoided any damage to important files. You also now know an Internet address that you will avoid in future and will advise others to avoid.

Secure actions

The whole basis of the Internet is that information is passed from one computer to another, so that security of information is much more difficult, since anyone along the way can look at data. For much of the information that passes, this is not a problem; it is, in fact, the way that the Internet was designed to be used, with access for everyone to the information. This free access, however, is less welcome if you want to use the Internet to transmit confidential information, particularly for items such as credit-card numbers, details of bank accounts, tax codes, etc. Because the Internet is increasingly being used for such confidential transactions, the most recent software, such as Microsoft Internet Explorer, contains security coding software, and other methods of ensuring security are also used.

Essentials of computer security

One system is the use of secure sites, meaning Internet sites that are equipped with security software. Internet Explorer 3.0 (IE3) allows you to use these sites so that you can send data to and receive data from such sites. While you are using such a site, the toolbar of IE3 shows an icon of a padlock.

You can also opt for a warning from IE3 when you are about to take some action, such as sending your credit card number to an insecure site, that might cause your security to be breached. In addition, IE3 can warn you that a site is not secure, even if the site makes claims to be secure.

Another security system used by IE3 is certification. A personal certificate is one that relates to you as an Internet user, and would typically consist of your name and a password that you set for yourself. This certificate would be used when a site demands some evidence of your status. The other type of certificate is the Web site certificate. Such a certificate is issued to a site for a limited period, and the certificate data can be recognised by IE3 when you make contact with that site. If the correct certificate data is received, and is not out of date, IE3 will proceed with the contact, otherwise a warning will be displayed. This is intended to ensure that a site is genuinely what it claims to be.

In addition to these measures, IE3 allows the use of security systems called SSL2, SSL3 and PCT for the highest levels of security that are currently attainable. These are supported by Web sites that offer secure transactions, and are considered to be secure enough for credit-card transactions.

Email

Email is another area that has attracted attention in the past, with newspaper reports of messages being left in the Email box of the Duke of Edinburgh. That is not really hacking; it's on a par with finding someone's telephone number and

On-line security

ringing up their answering machine. The point of Email is that it exists as a file on some remote computer until you read it in. If all you get is a message then no harm is done unless you dislike the message. It's quite another matter if the Email contains a program as an attachment, and the advice on not running programs from an unknown source applies also in this case.

Your Email address is not intended to be a secure item, and is even less secure than your telephone number. Your telephone number is printed in the directory, but your email address can often be guessed without resort to any form of directory, because Email addresses are meant to be easy to remember, and they all take the same style, which consists of your name, followed by the @ sign, and then the name of the Email providing service. If you know what providing service a company or an individual uses, you can often guess the full Email address without much bother. For example, if we have a (fictitious) provider called pullpop.co.uk, and you know that a Mr. Joe Soap is on Email with that provider, then you can try Email addresses such as joe.soap@pullpop.co.uk, ringing the changes on the first part, such as jsoap, j.soap and so on until your message is sent. This makes it equally easy for anyone else to send you a message, and that, after all, is what the system is for.

7 Viruses

A virus is defined as a program (which can include a macro written for a word processor or spreadsheet) that attaches itself to other program files and replicates itself so that it will be spread when programs are passed from one user to another.

The effects of such a virus can range from a message of the 'Kilroy was here' variety through corruption of screen images, all the way to corruption of a hard drive and destruction of files. Anti-virus software, (a *vaccine*), can be of some use, but the only certain way of avoiding a virus is to be sure that all programs that are loaded into the computer come from reputable sources. This often amounts to a matter of office discipline, because if staff members can bring in programs on floppies and run them in office hours, things are just too lax. Like hacking, virus fear is often unnecessary, and if you are running a stand-alone computer with software bought from respectable sources, with no access to outsiders, you are most unlikely to contract a virus.

Hard drive viruses, then, are a menace which affect very few hard-disc users, but which, like hacking, cause more worries and expense than damage. The term 'virus' should, strictly speaking, be applied only to a piece of code which can attach itself to a program and reproduce itself so that it can be transmitted to other programs and also from one computer to another. The term is, however, also used of other unwanted codes which can be loaded into a computer and which from then on will cause problems to appear, whether these can be spread to further computers or not.

The main types of virus are the *Boot Sector* type which locates itself in the boot sector of the hard disc and loads in whenever the computer is booted, and the *Parasitic* virus, which is attached to a program file and is activated when that

Viruses

program is used. The boot sector type of virus is estimated by one authority to account for 80% of all reported viruses.

The problem is not one that affects the few remaining machines that run only floppy discs, because a floppy disc with a virus can be thrown away. You can hardly throw away your hard disc if it is infected. A virus is also less likely to affect machines that obtain programs through a network and have no floppy drive fitted, because on such networks, only the server will have a floppy drive and access to the server can be more closely secured.

Viruses are not effective on data files, because data files are not composed of instructions, so that the virus instructions cannot be executed. Virus code in a text file, for example, would appear as gibberish that you could delete from the file. See, however, the note at the end of this chapter on a type of macro that has appeared on documents for Word for Windows.

The fundamental points are:

- A virus can affect your computer only if you load and run a program from a disc that contains the virus, or load and run software of unknown quality over the telephone lines by way of a modem.
- Millions of computer users who do not use a modem and are careful about where they buy software are at no risk of virus infection.
- Many viruses are comparatively harmless, like graffiti, and have been devised by programmers wishing to demonstrate their skills.

Essentials of computer security

Virus types

The *Trojan Horse* is not really a virus, but it can cause just as serious problems. It takes the form of a program with an interesting title. When the program is loaded and run, it carries out the damage. There is no subtle corruption here, and the user has done the damage just by succumbing to curiosity. This reinforces the importance of using only software that has come from respectable sources. It also points to the wisdom of not having floppy drives on networked computers in offices.

The *Worm* is also not really a virus but it reproduces itself within the computer that it affects until so many copies have been made of the code that there is no further room on the hard disc. It also has a serious effect on networks. This is a nuisance which can be fairly easily dealt with.

The true virus will attach itself to programs that you use, and if these programs are copied to other computers this will allow the virus to be spread. This type of virus may in some forms be comparatively harmless, but some very nasty varieties exist which can cause files to vanish from your hard disc directory. This damage is not necessarily irreversible, but even if it is not it can take a long time to sort out. The really destructive viruses are fortunately rare.

Always be suspicious about unsolicited gifts of discs such as demonstration discs. If in doubt, try them on an old floppy-only machine. Discs that have been run in a large number of machines are also suspect, as they could have picked up a virus from an infected machine. Programs on the Internet are also a prime possible source of viruses, and you should always question where a program has been obtained.

Another form of software war is the bomb. Bombs, also not necessarily viruses, come in two forms, time bombs and logic

Viruses

bombs. A bomb program, once loaded, saves itself on the disc and does nothing until some condition is met. A time-bomb will be activated by date (like Friday 13th) or time (like midnight) and will carry out its action if the computer is running at this time. A logic bomb will operate when some other condition is fulfilled, such as 65% or more of the disc being used, or a copy of some well-known program being installed. Software bombs are usually left inside computers by ex-employees, and they can be detected by inspecting the contents of AUTOEXEC.BAT or the Windows 95 Startup folder.

The earliest types of virus programs were comparatively simple. They usually altered the MS-DOS COMMAND.COM file, and could be counteracted by checking the size of this file regularly and re-installing if necessary. Later types of viruses are much more ingenious, using a variety of techniques to conceal their presence and to evade virus-detecting software.

The sequence of bytes that is used by viruses can often be used to detect a virus, and some now use code that is varied each time the virus reproduces. A few portions, however, need to be kept in sequence and can be detected. This, along with other data, forms the basis of programs which recognise and destroy viruses. Note however that no anti-virus program is nearly as effective as taking care not to become infected. In addition, anti-virus programs need to have their data refreshed at intervals to deal with new viruses that come along.

One problem that has complicated the virus war is that Windows 95, unlike Windows 3.1, did not initially contain any anti-virus software, and it has taken some time to develop anti-virus programs for Windows 95, all of which you must buy from other suppliers. If you use Windows 95 and you are concerned about a virus risk, you should buy reputable anti-

Essentials of computer security

virus software that is specifically intended for use with Windows 95. The description of the anti-virus programs for Windows 3.1, see later, illustrate the typical methods that are used by other anti-virus programs.

Avoiding infection

The problem needs to be put into perspective. I place several hundred floppies into my computer each year, and have never had a virus. No-one else uses my computer, I do not use a modem other than for fax and Email, and I get all my discs from the manufacturers. If your system is used like mine, you are not in danger.

The best method of dealing with viruses, computer or biological, is not to become infected. As far as your computer is concerned, you might not be in any danger. If you are in no danger it is pointless to expend cash and energy on a threat that does not exist.

Viruses reach your hard-drive either from a floppy disc that you have used to install something, or from a program that you have received by way of the modem, and subsequently run. Files that contain only data will not pass a virus, and programs that you run from a floppy and which do not install anything on the hard drive are also innocent. If in doubt, keep an old computer around which uses only a floppy drive (where are all these old Amstrads?) and use this to test any floppy disc that you have doubts about.

Beware of gifts of discs. Obtain programs only from reputable suppliers, whether these are commercial programs or shareware. Never run games programs that are passed on from another user. Beware also of demonstration discs or system checking discs that have been inserted into a large number of computers.

Viruses

One useful safeguard is to keep adequate backups of all program files and system files. If all else fails, you can wipe the hard drive and reinstall your system from backups. You should not, of course, attempt to make a backup when you suspect that you have contracted a virus, because this will compound the problem by infecting any drive that has files restored from the backups.

Windows 3.1 anti-virus

The MWAV program can be used from Windows as a way of checking for and deterring the entry of a virus. The files are not part of Windows 3.1 itself, but of MS-DOS 6.22, and when the computer had MS-DOS installed the Windows variety of anti-virus software, Microsoft Windows Anti Virus (MSAV) should have been installed. These programs, if they are on your hard drive, must not be used along with Windows 95.

There are two program files in the MWAV set, MWAV, which is the main virus checking file, and MWAVTSR, which is used to try to detect actions that might be introducing a virus.

The basis for detecting a virus being introduced is a change in a program file, or some 'signature' of bits appearing in a program file. Since new viruses are being invented and spread at frequent intervals, you need to keep an updated file of data as part of your virus scanning software. This, for the Microsoft anti-virus system for Windows 3.1, is the file MSAVIRUS.LST.

Detecting any attempt to install a virus is more difficult, because the actions that are used to install a program are also those that install a virus, but if you disable the detection when you are installing a legitimate program you should not be too troubled by false reports. You need also to maintain an up-to-

Essentials of computer security

date virus list. This can be updated by way of your modem. If you have no modem, that's one less reason to worry about viruses.

To use MWAV with Windows 3.1, double-click on the MWAV icon. You will see the MWAV panel appear, see below. Select the drive you want to scan by clicking on the drive icon — this will almost certainly be C:, but you might want to check a floppy in A: to find if it contains a virus before you copy its contents to the hard drive.

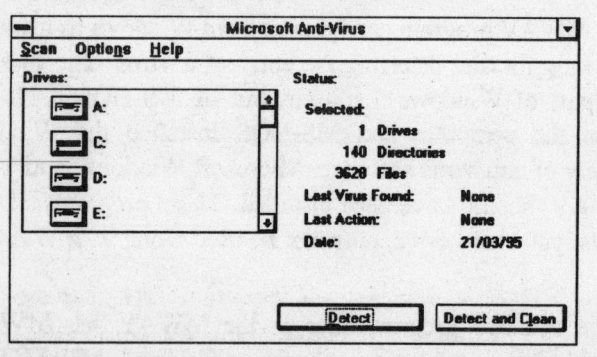

```
┌─────────────────────────────────────────────────┐
│  −           Microsoft Anti-Virus            ▼  │
│  Scan  Options  Help                            │
│  Drives:                  Status:               │
│   ┌──┐                    Selected:             │
│   │A:│                         1 Drives         │
│   │C:│                       140 Directories    │
│   │D:│                      3620 Files          │
│   │E:│                    Last Virus Found: None│
│                           Last Action:     None │
│                           Date:        21/03/95 │
│                                                 │
│              [ Detect ]   [ Detect and Clean ]  │
└─────────────────────────────────────────────────┘
```

You can now opt to use *Detect* or *Detect and Clean*. When you use *Detect*, you will see the memory scanned followed by a much longer scan for files. The files scan on a large hard drive can take a considerable time. Make a coffee and relax.

Normally you will see a report to the effect that all the files have been scanned and no contamination was found. This does not prove that your drive has no viruses, only that none have been found using this software. Unfortunately, not all anti-virus scans are equally efficient. You can find that a virus is reported where no virus exists, and, more seriously, that a real virus is not detected.

If the *Detect* scan reveals a virus, you can *use Detect and Clean* the next time round, and with luck this will eliminate the cause of the problem

Viruses

Remember that MSAV tries to identify viruses from its list of known types. You can click on *Scan* and then on *Virus List* to see (or print) the list of known viruses (see below). The names (and spelling!) tell an interesting story about the type of people who create these programs.

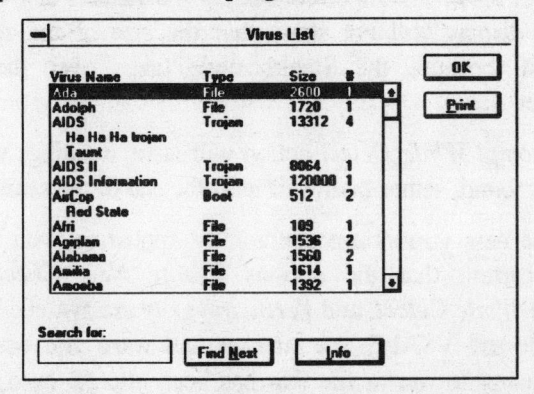

Virus Name	Type	Size	#
Ada	File	2600	1
Adolph	File	1720	1
AIDS	Trojan	13312	4
Ha Ha Ha trojan			
Taunt			
AIDS II	Trojan	8064	1
AIDS Information	Trojan	120000	1
AirCop	Boot	512	2
Red State			
Afri	File	109	1
Agiplan	File	1536	2
Alabama	File	1560	2
Amilia	File	1614	1
Amoeba	File	1392	1

MSAV contains a set of options, illustrated below. *Verify Integrity* sets up a check on program files that looks for changes and warns you. Note that this can cause false alarms on some programs that allow the main program to change when you alter your configuration settings. Later Windows 3.1 programs used an INI file for settings and do not change the main program file.

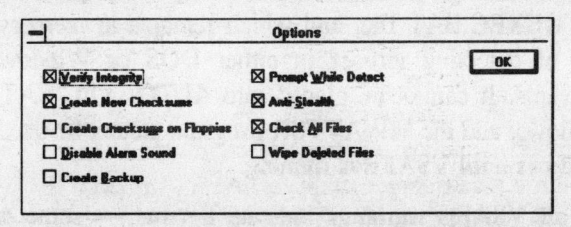

Options

- ☒ Verify Integrity
- ☒ Create New Checksums
- ☐ Create Checksums on Floppies
- ☐ Disable Alarm Sound
- ☐ Create Backup
- ☒ Prompt While Detect
- ☒ Anti-Stealth
- ☒ Check All Files
- ☐ Wipe Deleted Files

Several anti-virus methods rely on a checksum. This is a figure that is obtained from all the number codes in a file, and its merit is that any change in a file will affect the checksum if the checksum method is a good one. The option to *Create New Checksums* will in the course of a scan create a new

Essentials of computer security

checksum figure that can be used in future to check for any changes.

The *anti-Stealth* option should always be switched on. The Stealth type of virus is one that not only contains the virus itself but also methods of concealing the virus. For example, a DIR display will not show that the size of the file has changed, because the Stealth code takes over the DIR statistics.

The *Prompt While Detect* action will issue warnings when a virus is found, rather than wait until the end of the scan.

Because new viruses are continually appearing, you should make certain that the options *Create New Checksums, Prompt While Detect*, and *Verify Integrity* are switched on. If you also use VSAFE, see later, it will warn you whenever you attempt to run a file that has been altered, even if this alteration has not been caused by a virus.

If you want to see information on a particular virus, click its name in the Virus List

Using Vsafe

VSAFE is a program that is executed from the MS-DOS AUTOEXEC.BAT file, and which remains in memory as a way of detecting viruses in either DOS or Windows 3.1 programs. It cannot be placed into AUTOEXEC.BAT from Windows, and the MWAVTSR program cannot be used from Windows until VSAFE is running.

Not all VSAFE warnings indicate a virus — some can be triggered by perfectly legitimate actions. Only by knowing the normal behaviour of your computer can you sort out the normal from the abnormal. If you have been using VSAFE along with Windows 3.1, you must disable the program (by removing the VSAFE line from AUTOEXEC.BAT) before you install Windows 95.

Viruses in documents

A more recent form of virus is attached to documents, particularly to Word for Windows documents. Word allows a form of program, called a *macro*, to be attached to a document, and it is comparatively simple to write a virus in this form, so that clicking on an icon in the document will trigger the virus. Conventional virus scanning programs do not detect macros in documents and so ignore this form.

The main safeguard for Word users is not to click an icon in any document that you receive from an unknown source, either on disc or by way of a modem through the Internet or as an attachment in email.

Though the virus macro does not cause data loss, and does not infect other programs, it has a nuisance value; for example, the first variety to be detected saved all documents as templates, creating a glut of template files. Microsoft initially developed a detector for such macros using the Word document SCAN.DOC which contains a scanning macro. This document can be downloaded through the Internet site at http://www.microsoft.com/ by selecting "Microsoft provides fix for prank macro", and is available on some other Microsoft sites. Users of Word-7 for Windows 95 can obtain a free upgrade, Issue 7a, which incorporates a scanning system for all known macro viruses. By the time this book is in print, more advanced scanning tools will be available for dealing with corrupting macros.

8 Power supply interruption

Data at risk

We tend to take our mains electricity supply for granted, mainly because power interruption is rare and when it occurs, often predictable. If you live in a country district you will know to keep a torch handy when there is snow and high winds, and in these circumstances you would not normally be using the computer.

Power supply interruptions do not affect the data that is safely stored on the hard drive, and they certainly have no effect on data that is safely backed up. The only effect on a program occurs if you have changed the configuration of a program (such as altering the page size in Word) and the power fails before you can shut the programs down in the normal way. When power is restored and you re-start, the program will be in the same state as it had when you started it previously, with no configuration changes.

Loss of recent data is more serious. If, for example, you are working with a word-processor document, a worksheet, or a database, then the data you are entering from the keyboard is held only in the memory until it is saved. A power failure will wipe all the contents of the memory, and the only remedy is to type it all again when the power is restored — you have to hope that the supply will be restored for long enough to allow you to save your files this time.

If the data that you are entering is of considerable importance, and any loss is intolerable, you need to protect yourself against supply failure. For the less intensive computer user, backup methods may be sufficient, but for the commercial user the use of uninterruptable power supplies (UPS) is more appropriate. One simple solution is to enter all new data into a laptop running from its battery, but this is

Power supply interruption

appropriate only if battery maintenance is good. Another point is that a laptop is likely to cost more than a desktop machine plus its UPS.

Frequent backups

Frequent backing up is one way of avoiding the worst effects of supply failures. If you have an iron will, you might be able to remember to save your current data file every ten minutes or so, but it is much more likely that you will become so absorbed with entering the data that you will forget. If you have been typing for an hour or more when the power gives out you will have lost a lot of data, and it may not be easy to retype it just as it was.

Some programs are particularly helpful in this respect. Word for Windows has an automatic backup facility that can be switched on and set for whatever time interval you want to use. When this is on, an interruption to the power supply will stop the computer, but when the power is restored, Word will re-start with your document restored to the condition it was in when the last automatic backup took place. Note that this is not a *backup* in the sense used in Chapter 3, because only the hard drive is used.

Using such a system, you have to set the auto-backup time interval with some care. Using a very short interval will give better protection to your data, but your work will constantly be interrupted by the auto-save actions. Using a long interval creates fewer interruptions, but you might find that a power loss caused much more data to be lost. A setting of ten minutes is a good compromise for most users, and a shorter time can be used if you enter data at high speed.

Essentials of computer security

Uninterruptable power supplies (UPS)

An automatic backup will, at best, preserve some of the data you have been entering, but it does nothing to allow you to use the computer while the power supply is out. The aim of the UPS is to allow you to carry on using the computer for some time after a power interruption.

The basis of UPS is a unit which contains rechargeable batteries and which will automatically take over from the mains when the power supply fails. The transition is so fast that it has no effect on the computer, so that to all intents and purposes there has been no power failure to your computer. The obvious limitation is that batteries do not have an infinite capacity, so that the UPS will cease to be effective after some time. The more power your computer consumes, the faster it will drain the UPS batteries. Unless it is absolutely vital for you to keep computers working all through a supply failure, the UPS will normally supply power long enough for you to save all files, make backups and close down the system in an orderly way.

The rating of the UPS is indicated in a Volt-Amp (VA) figure, which should be large enough for your computer. This figure should exceed the rated power consumption in watts of your computer, so that if your computer uses 180 W then a UPS of 200 VA or more will be suitable.

Types of UPS.

The ultimate UPS, and the one that is required if a large number of computers must be kept working through a power failure, is a diesel generator which will start automatically when power fails. Because any such generator take some time to start, this system has to be accompanied by the electronic UPS units which will keep computers running until the

Power supply interruption

generator starts. Generator units are outside the scope of this book, because they are not exactly stock items for computer suppliers.

The electronic type of UPS which is stocked by a few larger computer suppliers, is a versatile unit that does rather more than simply take over when the mains power fails. The UPS is connected between the mains socket and the computer so that in normal circumstances the batteries of the UPS are kept charged and the mains supply is also filtered to remove surges, spikes (short-term excessive voltage) and line noise (high-frequency signals which can cause computer malfunction). When the mains power fails, the battery powers an inverter circuit which converts the low voltage DC of the battery into normal 230 V AC supply for the computer. This changeover is done in, typically, 2 thousandths of a second, ensuring that the computer has its power maintained (the computer would normally ignore an interruption of less than a quarter of a second).

The batteries that are used on UPS are normally the lead-acid type, since these are more reliable for this type of action than the nickel cadmium types (Nicad) that are used for portable computers and camcorders and most other rechargeable applications. Nickel cadmium batteries are excellent when they are in constant use, being discharged almost completely before re-charging, but for applications where batteries have to kept charged, and discharging is rare, lead-acid batteries are much better. The lead-acid batteries used for UPS are the sealed type which have a long life with no maintenance required.

The time for which the batteries can maintain power is typically from 5 to 15 minutes, depending on the rating of the UPS unit and the units it is required to supply. For example, the UPS might be used for the main computer and monitor only, ignoring printers, modems, scanners and other

Essentials of computer security

peripherals. The units contain warning signals that indicate when mains power has been lost and when battery power is almost exhausted.

Prices range from around £75 to more than £1500 depending on the power rating of the computer equipment the UPS is intended to protect. Buying such supplies is often difficult because retailers seldom keep any information leaflets, and you will need to find manufacturers or importers to get any useful information on the facilities that are available. Note that the use of lead-acid batteries makes the larger varieties of these units very heavy, so that carriage is costly and they cannot easily be moved around the office.

Appendix A

Hard drive data recovery

If a hard drive has failed before you have been able to back up all of its data, all is not necessarily lost providing that the failure is not mechanical. If the drive motor is still capable of spinning the platters and the head can still be moved across the platters, then data can be recovered even if the directory display show no files or folders or only gibberish. Such a failure is common when a head crash has wiped out the essential data that indicates how the files are stored on the drive, but your own data files may still be in reasonable condition.

Recovery, complete or partial, of data may be possible by software methods, using utilities for reading a drive directly. Such utilities need to be used by someone with some knowledge of disc drives and some experience with the software, but such people are not so rare as you might think, and many enthusiasts have such knowledge and experience.

Typical utilities for disc reading are available from Symantec (the Norton utilities and PC Tools) and can be bought from most retailers. Prices are of the order of £70 to £85.

If a hard drive has failed mechanically, so that the platters do not spin, or the head cannot move, any DIY solutions are ruled out. This does not mean that data recovery is impossible, but that it will be costly, as the drive will have to be dismantled in a dust-free laboratory and either the damage repaired, or the platters moved to a temporary drive so that data can be read and backed up to tape or to another hard drive. There a few specialists who will undertake this work, and names are listed in Appendix B.

Essentials of computer security

Appendix B

Specialists

The following firms specialise in the services indicated, and have been involved in these services for some time. Remember that some of these services are expensive, so that they have to weighed against the value of your data. On the other hand, the price may make you aware of the value of good backups in the future.

Always telephone an enquiry first, to make sure that the firm is still in business.

Physical security

Newland Design Ltd., Whitecross, Lancaster LA1 4QX Tel: (01524) 63221	Anti-theft alarms for PC machines, also effective against chip theft
Secura Systems, PO Box 7410, London N8 7NY Tel: (0181) 341 5089	Anti-theft alarms
Checkpoint Ltd., PO Box 31, Bristol BS15 1AR Tel: (0117) 961 1495	Alarm system for PC

Data recovery

Authentic Data Recovery, Tel: (0800) 581263	Recovery of data from crashed hard drive, unreadable floppy or dead

Appendices

fileserver. No fix. no fee basis.

Other

MAPEJ, | Specialises in transferring data between different and incompatible disc formats and/or sizes. Can also undertake text and image scanning to files
Meadow View,
Quinta Crescent,
Weston Rhyn,
Oswestry, Shrops,
SY10 7RN
Tel: (01691) 778659

CopyMaster (UK) Ltd., | Provides duplication services for copies to disc, tape or CD.
Caps Wood Business Centre,
Oxford Road,
Tatling End, Denham,
Bucks. UB9 4LH
Tel: (01895) 833 833

Essentials of computer security

Appendix C

Anti-virus software for Windows 95

The following anti-virus software is currently advertised for Windows 95. Not all such software is equally useful, and for commercial purposes, regular updating of virus lists is particularly important, as is a supplier who can help in difficult cases. This applies to the S&S International systems, marketed as Dr. Solomon's Anti-virus, which have been outstandingly successful over as long as virus problems have been around. Prices quoted below are 'street prices' from magazine advertisements, and include VAT.

Title	Price
Dr. Solomon's Anti-virus Toolkit - WIN95	£81.08
Symantec Norton Anti-virus Win95	£49.35
McAfee Virus Scan Classic Quarterly	£39.95

Index

INDEX

[+] sign, Backup, 24
air-conditioning, 1
alarm inside computer, 11
alarm systems, 11
alarms, flood, 8
allocation units, 14
alternative location, restoring, 31
anti-virus programs, 79
archival storage, backups, 56
audible prompts, Backup, 29
automatic backup, 87
automatic sprinklers, 9
avoiding virus infection, 80
backing up on floppies, 20
backing up, power failure, 87
backup, 20
Backup (Windows 95), 22
backup catalogue, 36
backup computer, 59
backup destination, 25
Backup panel, 24
backup storage, 55
backup, defence against virus, 81
backups, 3
bad portions, hard drive, 14
basement site, 8
Bernoulli drive, 42
bolting down, 11
bomb, 78
Boot Sector virus, 76
cartridge, QIC, 43
catastrophic failure, 47
CD-ROM, 5, 20

certification, Internet, 74
checksum, virus detection, 83
chip theft, 10
CHKDSK, 13
Colorado Jumbo, 43
Colorado Jumbo drive, 23
Compare options, 32
Compare tab, 28
comparison test, 52
compressed backups, 23
computer site, 7
computer theft, 2
computers in offices, 2
computers on line, 7
confidential information, Internet, 73
configuration test, 34
configuring MWBACKUP, 34
corrupted software, 1
corruption, 5, 13
crime prevention, 2
cross-linked files, 13, 16
customized programs, 3
damaged file, 16
damaged software, 1
DAT drive, 48
data cable, tape drive, 45
Data Compression, 31
data files, 20
DC2120 tapes, 47
dedicated data line, 70
defragmentation, 19
demonstration discs, 78
diesel generator, 88
disc maintenance, 13

95

Essentials of computer security

distributing copies, 59
Drag and Drop options, Backup, 33
drive bay, 45
drive deterioration, 14
DriveSpace, 22
elaborate passwords, 67
electronic UPS, 89
Email, 74
encrypting password, 72
external hard drive, 42
false alarms, virus, 83
FAT, 16
fax machines, 10
file cannot be read, 5
file condition, Windows 3.1, 64
file erasure, 60
File filtering, Backup, 33
File Manager, 21
file repairs, 14
file set, 26
filename, backup, 25
filtered power supply, 89
fire, 2, 9
fixing screws, tape unit, 46
flammable items, 9
flood alarms, 8
flooding, 8
floppy drive unavailable, 29
fluctuating magnetic fields, 4
fragmented file, 13
Full backup, 30
Full System Backup, 26
games programs, 80
generating password, 68
gifts of discs, 80
good password, 68

grandfather, father, son principle, 4
guessing passwords, 66
hacker, 66
hacking, 6
hard drive, 2
hard drive failure, 58
hard drive maintenance, 5
hard drive theft, 12
hard-drive crash test, 52
high-capacity floppies, 40
home computers, 3
ID number, SCSI, 41
identification stripe, data cable, 45
immunity from hacking, 68
Incremental backup, 30
inside information, 11
installation program, tape drive, 46
insurance, 2
internal security, 70
Internet, 72
Internet Explorer 3.0, 74
interval, auto-backup, 87
inverter circuit, 89
IR detectors, 11
irreplaceable software, 1
ISDN lines, 70
Jaz drive, 43
laptop, power failure precaution, 86
last floppy, Backup, 28
layers of trust, 12
lead-acid batteries, 89
level of protection, MWUNDEL, 65
log files, tape drive, 47

Index

logic bomb, 79
long-term storage, backups, 56
lose data, hard drive, 6
loss of files, 3
loss of recent data, 86
lost clusters, 13
macro, 21
macro virus, 76, 85
magnetic discs, 4
magnetic field hazard, 4
magnetic fields, 57
magneto-optical discs, 51
magneto-optical storage, 50
maintenance, hard drive, 6
marking chips, 12
memory theft, 12
modem, 6
monitor fire hazard, 9
MWAV program, Windows 3.1, 81
MWBACKUP, 33
MWUNDEL program, 63
network, 7
network server on line, 69
newspaper premises, 10
no-smoking rule, 9
off-the-shelf programs, 3
on-line security, 66
optical backup, 56
Optical storage, 49
options, Backup, 28
overwrite file options, 32
Panasonic mechanism, 51
Parasitic virus, 76
password storage, 71
password, generating, 68
passwords, 67
phase-change drive, 50

PIN number, 72
post-code mark, 12
power connector, 46
power supply interruption, 86
prank macro, 85
premiums, insurance, 2
printer port connection, 42
processor theft, 12
programs on floppies, 76
progress, Backup, 26
QIC extension, 26
QIC tape, 43
RAID system, 54
Recorder, 22
recovering information, 19
recovery, Backup, 27
recovery, corrupted file, 5
Recycle Bin, Windows 95, 61
reliability, hard drive, 6
removable hard drive, 42
replacing hard drive, 54
restore first character, 64
Restore options, 31
Restore tab, 27
retrieve deleted file, 61
scan, virus, 82
SCANDISK, 13, 15
SCSI interface, 41
secure sites, Internet, 74
securing computer room, 10
security coding software, 73
security review, on-line, 69
security systems, Internet, 74
selecting a folder, Backup, 25
Send To folder, 21
sensitive data, 1
Sentry, Windows 3.1, 65
settings, Recycle Bin, 62

Essentials of computer security

short-term security, 55
signature, virus, 81
simple backup, 21
slow failure, hard drive, 6
smoke and fire alarms, 9
spare backup drive, 60
status log, 29
Stealth virus, 84
storage of data, 4
storage space criteria, 57
strict grandfather – father – son system, 20
system checking discs, 80
System disc, 47
tape drive, 23
telephone networking, 68
testing backup system, 52
theft, 10
thorough scan, 16
time, UPS power, 89
time-bomb, 79
total loss, 2
Tracker, Windows 3.1, 65
Travan drive, 44
Travan tape units, 47
Trojan Horse virus, 78
type of backup, 30
ultra-violet pens, 12

unattended computer, 69
unattended equipment, 9
unauthorised copying, 7
un-deletion of files, 61
uninterruptable power supplies (UPS), 86
unsolicited gifts of discs, 78
UPS system, 88
using passwords, 71
utility programs, 6
vaccine, 76
value of backups, 55
VCR backup, 49
Verify backup, 31
virus, 73, 76
virus list, 82
virus-detecting software, 79
visible computers, 2
Volt-Amp rating, 88
VSAFE, Windows 3.1, 84
water authorities, 8
Web site certificate, 74
Windows 3.1 backups, 33
Windows 3.1 undelete, 63
Windows 95 anti-virus, 79
Worm virus, 78
Zip disc capacity, 41
Zip drive, 41